‘Poet, Paul Robert Mullen, explores deeply p
separations in order to find a true sense of self, explore the importance of memory and reflection, and find peace in settling for something new. His style is fractured, like the narratives running throughout, offering more implications than definitions.’

Cathleen Miller
International best-selling American author of *Desert Flower* and *Champion Of Choice*

‘Paul’s deft, sparse poems, like winter trees, stand stark against what might be sunrise or sunset, but offer an assured, quiet voice, in a variety of moods, not all elegiac. Their artifice is worn lightly, in line break and lineation, in apposite image: you can feel those ‘spider-web-december snowflakes’.’

Robert Sheppard
British poet, critic, author of *Twentieth Century Blues Empty Diaries, Warrant Error* and *Tin Pan Arcadia*

‘Mullen’s poems paint beautiful, devastating portraits of heartbreak and holding. These illuminated poems are powerful examples of craft and intent; the space created, a landscape of memory shared.’

Alexus Erin
American poet, author of *St. John’s Wort* and *Two Birds, All Moon*

‘As is true of all of his work, Mullen’s speakers find poetry itself to be salve, not necessarily because it’s cathartic, but because poetry is life.’

Kate Evans
Award-winning poet, memoirist, author of ***Call It Wonder: an odyssey of love, sex, spirit and travel*** **and** ***Wanderland: living the traveling life***

‘Mullen’s poetry is there to behold - engrossing because he creates a language for pain and sorrow that is uniquely his own: ‘the rust upon my heart strings / in A minor’. His poems ache, are economical, terse in form, mirroring the instant, hammer-to-the-heart pain of breakup and those causes.’

David Hanlon
Welsh poet, author of ***Spectrum Of Flight*** **and** ***Dawn’s Incision***

‘Mullen’s lens puts relationships, landscapes, current events, and even the past at arm’s length, letting the reader graze his poems with the tips of their fingers. The tactile nature of the images in this book tells a story of deep knowing, expectation, and even maybe a tinge of regret.’

Sage Danielle Curtis
American poet, author of ***Trashcan Funeral***

it's all come down to this: a retrospective

selected poems & writings
(1999-2024)

Paul Robert Mullen

Also by Paul Robert Mullen

Poetry Collections

Issues, Tissues & the Senseless Comic (2001)
curse this blue raincoat (2017)
testimony (2018)
35 (2018)
disintegration (2020)

Collaborations

Belisama (2021)

it's all come down to this: a retrospective

selected poems & writings
(1999-2024)

Paul Robert Mullen

The Broken Spine

it's all come down to this: a retrospective

selected poems & writings
(1999-2024)

Paul Robert Mullen

Brought to you by The Broken Spine

Art and Literature

ISBN:9798322485582

Book design: Alan Parry and Andrew James Lloyd
Cover Image: Thomas Clayson
Back Cover Image: Thomas Clayson
Cover Composition: Andrew James Lloyd
Line Drawings within the book: Emily June Kelly
Edited by Alan Parry

The Broken Spine Ltd
Southport / England / United Kingdom
www.thebrokenspine.co.uk

'...loneliness is a crowded room,
full of open hearts turned to stone,
all together all alone...'

Bryan Ferry & Roxy Music
Dance Away

contents

from a son to his Mother
[2013]

testimony
[2014-2016]

b-sides
[1999-2017]

disintegration
[2019-2020]

Belisama
[2021]

lockdown suburbia
[2020-2022]

fragments
[1999-2024]

1

preface

The artist is a curious creature.

Anyone with a propensity to create has challenges that inhibit their art. In my case, years in the wilderness, neglecting the thing I love to do most - *write.* Vast stretches of time evaporated without any recognisable artistic trace. Watching the years turn like a wheel, and just keep turning. Eventually it fills you with a sense of urgency … or immediacy … or even panic. You have to complete your art, otherwise it'll eat you from the inside out.

It's a monster that you need to dispel.

Skin that you must shed.

And then, other challenges. Lost manuscripts. The single most damaging and wounding blow to a writer. All that time, craft, thought, imagining. Gone, because I'm a tech novice with no patience. Because of neglect for an old machine when a new job finally saw me 'upgrade' to an Apple Mac. Technology versus the artist - an age old conundrum.

I should've kept notebooks, I'd curse myself.

I should've.

Covid-19. The most absurd, controversial and dramatic period of history since 9/11, where the world shut down and the very real horror of an impending apocalypse danced off the pages of science fiction and into all of our lives. An ideal time to create, which I did, but we were all preoccupied with something much greater and darker and more profound. Those few years are a blotch on everyone's copy book, not least mine.

And yet, here I am. Here *we* are. The battle against the elements in finally bringing this collection to light. A culmination of twenty-five years - a quarter of a century's worth of words and lines and messaging and metaphor. A lifetime within two covers. I don't know what it all means, to me or to anyone else. I don't suppose it matters. There might just be something in here that's relatable, or stimulates action, or provokes thought, or makes someone smile, jerks an emotion, or captures the imagination.

Voltaire said: 'The secret behind being boring is to say everything.' Everything being said, I hope I'm not so boring. Words are free, after all, but there's a price to be paid with what you say.

Twenty-five years cannot be easily explained. The difference between me as a wide-eyed sixteen year old teenager and a vastly experienced forty-one year old man lies on these pages. I first began writing when I went to college - part of an awakening that I attribute to reading. Before the age of commonplace mobile phones and the internet, I was a voracious reader. Every night before bed, every time I sat on a bus or train, walking down the street, Sunday afternoons, under the table during school lessons I wasn't fond of.

By that age I was devouring Charles Bukowski, Ernest Hemingway, Carol Ann Duffy, Leonard Cohen - not all poets, but poetic without question. When I went off to university in Sheffield the canon exploded. Lee Harwood, John Ashbery, Sylvia Plath, E.E. Cummings, Samuel Beckett. Writers that activated the kaleidoscope. Lyricists too, like Bob Dylan, Kate Bush, John Lennon, Joni Mitchell, Paul Simon. It was all starting to bubble and spit forth ideas and propositions that would, in time, become the words and the lines and the stanzas that make up this book. That wonderful, indescribable, ethereal, exciting, sensitive melting pot made up of flesh, bone, experience and influence.

A poet is a complex mind. Often wrapped up in webs of our own doing, we seek to unravel ourselves with explanations that, often, we're not prepared to deliver with any sort of direct and immediately decipherable intention. It's a never-ending web, in truth.

A therapy of sorts.

A necessity for most.

If it's not, then the heart probably isn't entirely in it. I could be wrong, of course.

That's just my point of view.

*

This book spans ten collections of work, some of which has been reimagined. A poem is never truly finished, and a poet never truly satisfied. The great and late Archie Markham - Montserratian poet, playwright, novelist and academic - told me that once after a lecture in Sheffield. I never forgot it.

Eight of those are solo collections - four of which have been published, one self-published back in the early days, and three as yet unreleased.

One collection was released independently with a very short run (*Issues, Tissues & the Senseless Comic* [2001]), three on American Press, Coyote Creek Books (*curse this blue raincoat* [2017], *testimony* [2018] and *35* [2018]), and one chapbook with Australian-American publishers, Animal Heart Press (*disintegration* [2020]). During this time I wrote a very personal collection called *from a son to his Mother*, but have yet to brave putting that out in full, despite interest from publishers. Poems from that collection feature in this book.

The poems span a long period of time - over two decades, and as aforementioned, began life in my college and university years, though the pen continued to be a sound companion throughout a long stretch of travelling the world. I spent significant amounts of time in Australia, lived and worked in China for over four years, and covered large parts of Asia (including North Korea) and vast amounts of Europe. The poems never stopped, and neither did I. I lived, loved, listened and watched it all happen in front me, breathing those incredible experiences in with scribbles on napkins and diary entries and phone notes and late-night scrawlings in dozens of half-full jotters. 'Write drunk', Hemingway said, 'and edit sober.'

Interestingly, *Belisama* [2021] was a collaboration with three fellow Southport dwellers and talented writers, Alan Parry (co-founder of The Broken Spine Artist Collective), local historian turned poet, David Walshe, and perceptive wordsmith, Mary Earnshaw. We put the collaboration together on a whim, and won a competition with Scottish press, Dreich, resulting in the collective publication.

The introduction to the *Belisama* collaboration notes the following:

> *Ptolemey's Geography from the second century of the Christian era locates Belisama in an area that has in the past been regarded as the River Ribble's environs, the River Mersey's environs, or the area in between. It is now regarded as describing a larger Ribble Estuary, close to where it joins the Irish Sea - in other words, the location of present day Southport.*

A worthy project, it fulfilled and illuminated a piece of my personal history - the place I grew up, went to school, and had all of my formative experiences -

Southport, the end of the Northern Line out of Liverpool. I thank Jack Caradoc for taking care of my - of *our* work.

There are poems in here from a collection that I abandoned, called *B-sides.* These poems were written in 2017 during my travels throughout Thailand, Vietnam, Laos and the Philippines. It was a time when I realised my time in China was probably coming to an end, so I was making the most of the surrounding areas of South-East Asia whilst based in that part of the world. I was frequenting hostels at that point in my life, not because I couldn't afford better, but because I found these places a great source of inspiration and joy. You could go from being a stranger to being sat amongst a group of new 'friends' from all over the world within minutes. The amount of super-interesting people I met in these places, the conversations I had, the drinks we shared, the fun times we managed to craft - it was great. A cultural cauldron of sorts. Everything was thrown in the mix, but what prevailed was a common and shared humanity. You could be sitting round a table with a Mongolian, two Chinese, a Canadian, someone from Switzerland, a Colombian, a Spaniard, three Kenyans and a Swede, and yet everyone would be laughing and chatting and learning and loving.

So, these poems were largely written in cafés and coffee houses 'the morning after.' A delicate breakfast, coffee, a view of the ocean, and some quietude would often fill my notebooks for me. Being in unfamiliar places is a great way to explore your true, inner feelings. I've no real reason why these poems were put on the backburner. Consequence of a scattered mind and a propulsion to pursue the immediate and forget about the past, probably.

The next batch of poems in this collection are from the second unreleased collection, *lockdown suburbia*, written throughout the obscene and unforeseen lockdown during the great pandemic, Covid-19. This project was commissioned by *Heart of Glass* as part of *Home Work*, with support from Cultural Hubs: St Helens Arts in Libraries, The Bluecoat, Knowsley Council, Rule of Threes, Sefton Council, Human Library, The Atkinson, Halton Borough Council, and Culture Liverpool. This was a particularly productive but dysfunctional time for me, and I was widely published in magazines, e-zines, anthologies and journals throughout this period without really having any direction. I had become nocturnal, as I'm sure many had. 4am became the new 11pm. Here I present a selection of those poems - my personal favourites, and reflections on that most improbable time in history.

This collection also features *fragments* - bits and bobs and odds and ends from the entire scope. Stuff that may have been published along the way but didn't make the collections, or might have been sitting in a drawer for years. I look at them like rare rediscoveries - studio recordings locked in a cupboard for years, if an analogy is needed. These can often be the most intriguing.

The final instalment is titled: *rags of light: new & unreleased poems*. This comprises mostly brand new works written specifically for this collection, and includes the poem of epic length, *vinyl redux.* This is arguably my most important instalment in this whole collection because it has offered me a way back into poetry after what felt like an irrecoverable wilderness.

I've been away from the scene and at odds with my writing for a long time.

Completing this career spanning body of work - *it's all come down to this: a retrospective [poems & writings (1999-2024)]* - was a struggle, but one that was entirely necessary and ultimately very relieving, if not also satisfying and illuminating.

I'd like to thank Alan Parry for his patience and continued efforts with the brilliant project that we set up, *The Broken Spine Artist Collective*, and his belief in my work. I'd also like to thank Kate Evans, a constant source of inspiration, support and poetic advice during my time on the road, and Matthew MC Smith, editor of *Black Bough Poetry*, for his generous editorial eye over some of these poems in their early forms. Cheers to Elisabeth Horan, Amanda McLeod and Beth Gordon for their trust in my very personal work with *Animal Heart Press*, and Jan McCutcheon of *Coyote Creek Books*, who took on my projects whole-heartedly.

Thanks to the great British poet and critic, Robert Sheppard, who I studied under and befriended during a particularly exciting, creative period of my life. He was Professor at Edge Hill University when I first got to know him, and I'm a great admirer of his work, erudition and artistry. Robert has provided an enormously insightful and typically punctilious, methodical, innovative and acute introduction. It's really a thrill and privilege to have someone so well renowned, and such a brilliant poet, analyse my work, as he has with two exceptional writers before me - Roy Fisher and Lee Harwood.

Emily June Kelly has provided some wonderful illustrations to complement the sections within this book, and bring to life my odes - and with that description I don't mean by structure - to some of my biggest inspirations. Unsurprisingly, Cohen, Dylan and Hemingway are all master wordsmiths in their respective fields - of course, Hemingway with the novel, Dylan with song lyrics, and Cohen, rather magically, with both of those disciplines, plus poetry. Miles Davis is a master of imagery in a different sense. He's the man that painted 'blue' into jazz. As Richard Williams documented in his book *The Blue Moment*, '[as a result of Miles] ...blue, the colour of heaven and of despair, of distance and intimacy, offers no easy resolutions.' Emily June Kelly's attention to detail and ability to visualise symbolism within my work is undeniable.

I would like to thank Rhyannon Parry, Maria Brewster, and all at Heart Of Glass for their help, support, and guidance.

Peace and love to David Hanlon, Dave Rhine, Steve McKenna, Cathleen Miller, Fran Zinder, Adrian Gautrey, Chris Wilson, Paul Kappa, Brad Metzler, Judi Metzler … and anyone I may have missed over all these years that have in any way encouraged me, humoured me, listened to, read or critiqued my words.

Thank you.

I'd like to thank my family and friends for their constant support with all of my creative endeavours, which have often stood in the way of common sense.

I want to mention some of my great inspirations and influences that I've yet to reference, too.

Poets like Alfred Starr Hamilton, Theresa Lola, Sean O'Brien, Warsan Shire, Billy Collins, Andrew McMillan, Adrienne Rich, Brian Patten, Barbara Guest, James Schuyler, Kenneth Koch, Adrian Henri, Roger McGough and Frank O'Hara.

Writers like Martin Amis, John Fante, Ma Jian, Louis-Ferdinand Céline, Angela Carter, John Kennedy Toole, Ken Kesey, Stan Barstow, Alice Walker, Alan Hollinghurst, Truman Capote, Albert Camus, Jeffrey Eugenides, Bernadine Evaristo, Franz Kafka, Haruki Murakami, Vladimir Nabokov, Gregory David Roberts, Dai Sijie, Gwendoline Riley, Graham Swift, Cheryl Strayed, John Williams, John Hersey and Cathleen

Miller also require mention. This pantheon of artists I truly admire, and have taken great inspiration from.

Occasionally I like Morrissey too. I've never got over that lyric in that Smiths song: *There Is a Light That Never Goes Out* - it just said everything that needed to be said for me.

Thanks also to all readers who support little known poets. Art is not bound to those who are famous, and neither should it be.

So many have inspired these poems and stories, for better or for worse, and their names and faces and voices are hanging in that great old tree at the top of the hill in the depths of my mind. Introspection is often the best way to look outside yourself, beyond yourself, and into a brighter future.

That's what I think I've done.

That's what I hope I've done.

Thanks for reading my words.

They're just words, after all, and yet so much more.

Paul Robert Mullen

September 2024

introduction

This is My Story, This is My Song:
Introducing the Poems & Writings

I find the contemporary German lyric poet Lutz Seiler puts the matter better than I could: '"Everyone has only one song," said the writer Paul Bowles in one of his last interviews. (He was also a musician.) You recognise the song by its sound. The sound forms in the instrument we ourselves have become over time. Before every poem comes the story we have lived. The poem catches the sound of it. Rather than narrating the story, it narrates its sound.' This seems an apt way of talking about the poems of Paul Robert Mullen, where what he calls 'a lifetime between two covers' is transmuted into a song, a song that is intensely personal, though not necessarily flagrantly autobiographical, or where autobiography has become song, a distant echo of fact. Mullen no longer tells the story: he offers us that condensed sound, that song, that story of the sound of the poem. That is its artifice, of course, which I shall be examining below.

However, it is worth dwelling on the musical analogy. Like Seiler, commenting on Bowles, I can say 'Mullen is also a musician,' one who I have seen perform (and I possess his entertaining CD *Alchemy in the Garden*). Although I will pursue the metaphor of 'song' in relation to Mullen – he writes much of his music as part of that story of his life – it is important that he never confuses a song lyric for a poem (or vice versa). His songs are another story, and music is only part – an important part, as I shall show – of the story of his verse.

Seiler is careful to interpret his quotation from Bowles. 'Everyone has only one song' does not mean that a writer keeps on writing the same poem over and over (I think of those blues musicians who seemed to only have one tune), although repetition, or what Lee Harwood, one of Mullen's favourite authors who can be glimpsed in the poem 'the poet', calls more positively 'insistences', are obviously part of any narrated life-story, however much transposed into song. Seiler amends his source: 'More than anything, "Everyone has only one song" means that everyone has a song, and 'only one' means it's their own song.' Throughout the 400 pages of *it's all come down to thi*s, Mullen's 'insistencies' weave between different existential situations, take different poetic forms. 'The search for' this unifying song, Seiler reminds us, 'can take a long time', 'a lifetime' as Mullen says. 'Years of eavesdropping on the melodies of others – good to listen in to, but is it your own particular song? You could say: the poem is something that, of necessity, asserts itself through the life of its author, it is his song, his faith in an "absolute rhythm" that is his own personal rhythm.'

Although Seiler is here quoting Ezra Pound, I think the point is his own, one that clearly reflects the essential feel of Mullen's work, although his song is discernibly different in poetry and prose. 'The poem is something that, of necessity, asserts itself through the life of its author' is amply demonstrated by this wonderful collection.

I want to examine one short poem to show how story becomes song. A poem such as 'Southport', with its geographically precise location (or so we might think), leads us to expect certain things, but the poem itself withdraws much of the detail of experience. Some years ago critics were interested in how readers construct texts, detailing ways they have to fill in the gaps, or indeterminacies as they would call them. 'Southport' begins 'overlooking the dunes/ you whisper to me'; this offers some specificity of time and place and establishes what are too spectral to call 'characters', the relationship barely hinted at by the intimate act of whispering. What is whispered is enigmatic, to say the least: 'the rains must have/ killed her'. (I ask readers to imagine a context for this situated remark; you may come up with a surprising range of possibilities.) The response to this scrap of speech, if that's what the rest of the poem narrates, is abrupt and surprising: 'as/ i start the engine'. Oh, they are in a car, we might guess, but that is only a guess. The surprises are aided by careful spatial lineation; the lowercase 'i' (used throughout the collection) pushes the reader away from identifying with the experience. The poem is unfinished but complete, its emotion intense but hauntingly unlocatable. So many of the short poems share something of this artifice. Only the bare bones are offered, and people, even lovers, are presented in a singular phrase or a notable feature or emphatic action. The aesthetic withdrawal of the poem means it is clearly offering the sound of the song, not the story of the narrative.

Often the endings of poems enact a hangdog acceptance of a negative or transitory experience. Flick through this book and check the point. The poem that ends 'i stand in the kitchen naked/ sing for the joy of it all' is an exception (and it is instructive that singing is the uplifting activity here). Sometimes poems begin with startling dismissals: 'Life,' one opens, is 'a clumsy bag of borrowed time'. Disappointed lyric is the apposite form for the *lockdown suburbia* sequence. On 'day 18' Mullen observes (what else could he do but witness and record?) the 'guttural wheeze' from 'the bed of ICU'. By 'day 70' he's listing the books he's reading. By 'day 82' he becomes political, noting 'Boris Johnson's/ hair ablaze/ with dishonour & defeat'.

There are a number of extraordinary long poems in this book that often take a choral or anaphoric structure that enables Mullen to trail disparate perceptions, often joyful ones, through its network. Narrative is abandoned for nodal repetition. 'you are punctuated by' is a modified list poem that itemises, poeticises, the formative 'punctuations' of life: 'dancing girls/ cocks bulging in silky trunks' right down to 'bird eating goliath spiders in/ late-night doorways', as well as 'Samuel Beckett' and 'Leon Trotsky' who simply appear, as names, in isolated lines of their own. Often he uses imperatives in this form to engage with the reader.

There are various poems that allude to popular and other musics in the book, the works of Bob Dylan and Leonard Cohen in particular. The long poem 'curse this blue raincoat', a reference to one of L. Cohen's most affective, shattering songs, is an unusually highly-wrought poem, structured around the un-cursing chorus 'i pray', often the pleading 'i pray for a response', as in 'i pray/ for a response/ to this curious emanation/ we call beauty'. (Cohen could have written that!) However, the most extraordinary long poem is 'vinyl redux', a hymn to the diversity of popular musics, allusive to artist names and fragments of titles and lyrics of which most readers will recognise parts, but probably not all. The extraordinary thing is that we trust the poem to make its continuous song from these discontinuous fragments. Almost impossible to quote from (you have the whole of its 'curious emanations' ahead of you, gentle reader!) it climaxes with an acknowledgement of kinship with Marvin Gaye's seminal *What's Going On*? 'So mercy me/ hardly a dishonest note/ i just know this much/ is true,' Mullen concludes, bringing this epic to rest at a point where he has literally transposed the songs of our time into a truth. In more sense than one, 'The sound forms in the instrument we ourselves have become over time,' as Seiler puts it, and Mullen demonstrates this in his intense listening 'over time'. His prayers for a response have been answered.

Like many lyric poets before him, Mullen finds his poems writing about poetry itself. This happens many times in this collection, but one poem stands out, which has an appropriately musical context. 'some people have no poetry' alludes to the famous riposte of Bossa Nova genius João Gilberto to his psychiatrist, as he was counselled away from his 'fancy' that the wind outside the asylum window was 'brushing the hair of the trees'; it's just weather, the doctor assured Gilberto, speaking sane but limiting facts that are not to be confused with poetic truth. 'some people have no poetry' defines poetry as imaginative outwardness, while its lack is seen to engender polished but blind self-regard. It attempts to imagine the imaginative paucity of such an outlook: 'how do they look into/ the eyes/ of another/ & see anything but/ themselves?' Again, we see the aesthetic truth succinctly encapsulated and condensed, that 'before every poem comes the story we have lived. The poem catches the sound of it.'

One final remark: there are a number of works of fiction that weave through the book, and that stay close to the story that Mullen has lived. In 'provincial town taxi rank' the approach of threatening bullies (a situation we find so often in the poems too that it feels existential) is related in all its horror. As they progress these prose pieces feel less like colourful autobiographical vignettes – though I did enjoy the seaside binge provocations of 'Blackpool' – until in 'death look' we have a fully-formed and absorbing fiction about a child with premonitions of others' deaths, a ghastly gift. These are the 'writings' of the subtitle: 'selected poems and writings 1999-2024', a title and dating that reminds us that that story that Mullen has lived is a long one. The sounds that he has made during, and from, that life, are often exquisite and always truly affective.

Robert Sheppard
June 2024

Work Cited

Seiler, Lutz. trans. Martyn Crucefix. In Case of Loss. Sheffield, London, New York: And Other Stories, 2023: 97.

a note from the editor

It is with the deepest sense of honour that I bring to your hands a collection of writing that provides a profound insight into the heart and mind of a writer I deeply admire and respect, Paul Robert Mullen. *it's all come down to this: a retrospective [poems & writings (1999-2024)]* is a journey through the innermost depths of a poet's soul, documented with complete candour.

Within these pages, you will encounter writings that have never before seen the light of day. These words, often tinged with lust, nostalgia and vulnerability, have been carefully preserved, awaiting the moment when they could be shared with the world. With *you*. These previously unpublished offerings serve to enhance other selected works from Mullen's significant writing career.

This book is an authentic testament to the incredible range of human emotions and experiences, brought to life by a poet who leaves nothing behind in his craft. It is a must-read for anyone who seeks to understand the intricate workings of the human heart and mind, laid bare on the page.

Mullen's literary journey spans over two and a half decades - a testament to his unwavering dedication to the craft.

Over the course of twenty-five years, Paul has knitted together emotions, reflections, and stories that resonate deeply. Indeed, what sets him apart is his incisiveness and fearlessness. His writing is not the work of a mere luminary; it's the product of a poet whose reading and rendering of people and the everyday is as perceptive as it is penetrative. In short, Mullen has lived, and this is evident in the work he produces.

Poems like, *call it wonder* and *aftermath* are more than verse on paper; they are prophetic windows. This work scrutinises, observes, transforms, questions and captures its subject with integrity and verisimilitude. Mullen clearly understands and takes his role as a poet seriously. His line, 'he was a poet - what a thing to be!' captures the essence of my admiration for his craft and the transformative effect his poetry has had on me.

Paul Robert Mullen's poetic career exemplifies the profound influence of the written word in inspiring, forging connections, and stirring our deepest emotions. I invite you to immerse yourselves once again in his work, to discover or rediscover the authenticity and emotional depth that only a true wordsmith can convey.

With profound admiration and respect,

Alan Parry
Editor-in-Chief
The Broken Spine
September 2024

Photo Credit: Gary Dougherty

24

Issues, Tissues & the Senseless Comic

[1999-2004]

fire

stricken
soul to skin

from within

smothered

stifled

*

indigo hue

death
where shadows unfold a vast canvas
an unknown passage

a blessing amidst

flames

ecstatic

beautiful

you can't ride the tide

reflections opaque   your face
      breaking into white
   moonlit night

it's so cold

midnight mists
   pathways dissolving

boundless clouds gathering waves
   they don't slither
         anymore

   instead they
      SCREAM

hisssssssss crash   retreat

& it comes again
      & again
   & again

the moon choked   muddied fog

   where's the shore?

the straight road

the map
will take you where
you need to go

to peace beyond hills

a shiver in your limbs
words upon tongues

a road of your own making

bridges to cross
staring into friends

down highways // past lakes
making love or war in
flower beds

gushing through fields in the rain

home, home, home

silhouettes

for Frank & Maureen Bolger

time passes a silent river
such swaying gentle brutality
roving current toward
bloom & decay

morning sun shimmies below dusk
minds at ease
they've seen it all

wisdom like lanterns
they know
they *know*

dawn settles on warm grass
rain beats slates like fists

kettle steaming // solid walls built
with graft & time
& compassion

scent of oven-baked
sausage rolls
& victoria sponge
Grandstand on the box

& love
the seeds of something unteachable
with words

unreachable with ambition
alone

unthinkable in dreams

remaining the same
when times change
when lives an uncharted display
are rearranged
in aeternum

vieux carré

we lie awake in New Orleans
tracking vivid dreams

the quarter is no life
          for me
it's where cards are dealt 'til
                    dawn
          where hours trample
                                        feeble wives

eyes upon a theatre stage
childhood horror
memories just dirty souvenirs
          rags & spades
east & west
sleeping on unmade beds

the search for love
                    & money
          & company

the trials that make up all we say

a drink
to start another day

premature

sunrise over fire

gold amongst agony

|

time a relentless sculptor
the hushed orchestrator

|

you were laid down

cheap

meaningless

young

gentle in the morning

the soft breeze quieter
than
silence

the secret garden

hot sick fantasies

an empty diary of its time

concealed skies
well groomed headlines
& everything breathes
like flushed alley-cats

voices purr eventually through
crisp stone

grasses sway like birds
stupefied // immaculate
palette pale & strange
the past laid out
in stereo

years taking leave through doors
without handles

without warning

contours

in the park
lying awake

this wilderness
a place to sanctify
rooftop of violent stars
exploding calm

wherever you are
however far
the wind in your sails
gathering daydreams
the price of losing just escape

&
didn't we nearly make it
like grapes on a vine
in a time before *this* time
when throats gripped
we walked tip-toe
to-&-fro
towards something more
or less

stuck on one side of both worlds

life
a clumsy bag of borrowed time

this body
complex sackcloth // spice & dust
loose at liberty
dragging through weary dog-tired
winters

naked electric truths
recalling friends // faces
murmurs in the underbelly
the past bowed on this hardened
horsewhipped
shoulder

our human shape
prick in hand
paranoid to fuck in mirrors
torn face // lean jeans
no surprises

eyes like children
lost // inferior

& the wind
        harsh // erotic
like unheard stab wounds

        ideas fatty like parasites
a swollen womb
smiling through it all
                & more

cyclone giggles
        …we all end up in the same place…

wandering into the woods
the place we'll
        meet your end
(in)discreetly

curse this blue raincoat

[2005-2012]

ex post facto

looking at that old man today
tired of life

&
in the same room
a young boy
full of life

i thought
i must be somewhere in between
staring out of the
window
into an empty
garden

the poet

we shuffled into the theatre
in twos & threes
sitting on numbing plastic with
        little leg room for
a tall guy like
        me

chattering & murmuring
in anticipation
        filling spaces
between gatherings
the air humid // an empty
                stage

& then the poet ambled in

small   gaunt
liver-spotted
        late 60's at a guess
bottomless eyes behind
                tinted lenses

renowned // distinguished
        but not
particularly famous

though i admired him without
        ever knowing him

he was a poet - *what a thing to be!*

he started to read
        under intense amber swell
soft // vulnerable
wearing lines like patches on
        his baggy sleeve

a poem about his Grandmother

he began crying
        all those years later
& my defences shattered right there

helpless to his words
hopeless to his tears

& the theatre
        held its breath

such *curious* words

last tuesday

the little girl just
started laughing
at the funeral
          heeheehee

then her Mother laughed too
though nervously
& it became contagious
spreading down the whole row
until ten people laughed
then twenty
thirty
madness in their eyes

& i couldn't stand it
anymore
so i left before they pushed him
          into the furnace
walked across town
placed a bet on the 3:10pm steeplechase
an outsider
which just felt good

          i got holed up
in a strip bar where i could free

my mind
of sickening laughter

three hours later
darkness had fallen with a bottle
          of the finest

i felt much better
& laughed out loud
          ha ha ha ha ha
since the horse
               came in
& i had scotch in hand
cash for the night
& nobody
          left to bury

sundown on the 68

there's needle in the night air
    of Manhattan

foreboding
like i've never known

& i see
danger in the haste of
        moving limbs
pounding through
shadows & fading silver
        main-street hustle

adolescent breaths of forming
    hurricanes sweeping folk into
        relentless scamper
    into the shallow sigh
            of twilight

& yet
between growing disarray
there's talk
    of Laurel Canyon
    & the daughter divine

then the quake
    of text vibration

    what will we have for dinner, honey?

    pasta? pizza?

    something quick....

clogged exhausts
& screaming child hungry
        for calm through
the steam & lurching
        superstructures
pressing on the skyline

the subways full
the bars full
the madhouses full
park benches draped in filthy
    rags
the lost & lonely pissing in
    the wind
        shameless

they've seen it all before
they'll see it all again

impoverished eyes
fixed
on their own glory
fixed
on the thick soup blazing wilderness
          of per diem
                    banality

Southport

overlooking the dunes
you whisper to me
the rains must have
killed her

as
i start the engine

midnight

looking out over the marina
          stoned

she asks
if i see the shark

she says it's beautiful
slicing through moonlit sonic
          flint & fog
          beside the jetty

i tell her i think so
                    sitting down

the voltaic neon fuzz
                    of the harbour

trying to focus on people

the people   trying to focus on
an inky shimmering
          ocean

          lost behind promenades
watching the people

& the waves
& the   people

             focus   trying
                                 on people
                                             on waves
rolling
in
& in
& in
      & out

mercy

standing over the fox
twisted fatal in wire
i see compassion in your eyes
        turn to tears

though i just can't
        end it
        the man that i am

    do it

        you say

just do it

country music

country music
she said
isn't complicated

    it will either make you laugh
    or break your heart

just like waking up in the morning
    i said

long hot summer

she went missing in summer
the girl with
        turquoise eyes
hottest summer
        for thirty years

that same summer his lilies bloomed
                early

they thought
        she'd ran away
driven mad by
        the full moon

they searched & searched
without trace

still
his lilies grew strong
        a wonderful pale cream
& he cared for them
sympathetically // slicing them from
        peppermint stalks with
            precision
placing them in cold water

with a thumbnail of
          sugar

for years
every sunday afternoon
he’d take two
          or three
to flower
where she lay

everywhere

i hear your voice
          everywhere i go

in the streets
in sewers
in the squeals of the cinders of
          the fiercest fires

inside walls
in lavatories // factories
trains & buses
alleyways // asylums
          & the cockpit flying
                    s
                     o
                      u
                       t
                        h

the courthouses
the entrails
          of the theatre pit

inside the fizz
          of champagne

& the minds of
          grand juries

you
are everywhere
to

          me

curse this blue raincoat

i pray
for a response to beauty
to the wonder
          in this landscape
in this being
in these entities

i pray
for a response
to this curious emanation
          we call beauty
this power in an untold vision
a touch
a breath of air on mountain tops
the complexion of the sky &
          the scent of a wildflower
the torment in the face
                    of the singer
whose passions have overwhelmed them
to the humility in genius
the cries of broken hearts in hell
the magnificence of
          new life & the miracle
                              of sexual union

i pray
for a response to thunder in
                                        the words of the poet
the blazing vivid lights when we
                    close our eyes
the wrinkles on your skin in the
                                                            dead of night
                    to those who rejoice as
                                        fires ravage the horizon
                    those who turn their back on
                                                            hope
                                        to winners & losers
                    the frenzied convictions of youth &
the words of the prophet

i pray
for a response to love &
                                                  friendship
to the privileges we are afforded in dark times
to passivity   curiosity
obsession & religious kitsch
                    to recklessness
falling rocks on the horizon
                    the oceans & smouldering summers
savagery in an honest tongue
the unacknowledged legislators of the world
the sensory overload of
                    the piano

jubilation hidden in the artist's brush
reflections in the window
   & to the labours that arise from
         loving

i pray
for a response to paradise
   to apathy
victory upon victory
to the young soul rebels
   the surrender to mediocrity
      those who play the heroes in
      their own drama
   life after death
comic strips   superheroes
the glory of the final hunt & birds of prey
to footfalls on the dancefloor
translations hidden in monasteries hidden
         in jungles
      hidden in notions & belief

i pray
for a response to the raven
         & the dove
   the naivety of age
      to big ideas in microscopic minds
the end of a night when starting the journey

evaporating popularity // increasing popularity
(evaporating … again)
to superstition
the condemnation of communism
our notion of forever
feral mortal sacrifice &
the quest for martyrdom

i pray
for a response to the march
the beating of the drum
the ringing of bells
to the zeppelin in flight heading
back to the end of the beginning
the backstreets of Paris in
summertime

to Krishna
the epic play
raised glasses in a tempest
the call of duty
liars in dimly lit subways
the embrace of rival armies
shared cigarettes after sex
to the tangled circumstances of existence &
crooked signs on
roads leading nowhere

i pray
for a response to your irrational love for
                    me & mine

i pray for wisdom
for the lonely unenterprising fool
the good old days &
          an inconceivable future
stigma   our eyes
the horn of the unicorn
sweeping echoes across the moors
the bruised fortunes of
                         doomed sailors &
the enigma of the Isrealites
to our mind-melting
          jobsworth colleagues who
chew at our souls &
the blackbirds
          balanced in silver beeches
                    ready to fly

i pray for a response to
                         the final supper
to those that suffer for their art
the sisters of mercy
to the summits & crests of
          the tsunami that crushes the harbours
                              of the world

to the heaviness in sharing
weakness in the eyes of the predator
the fury of the lion
rituals in forests &
the deepest of all thinkers
who carry such weight

i pray
for identity divinity
silhouettes in stark-raving moonlight
to the gurus & lessons learnt at dusk
warriors still battling already dead
the pin-drop in packed theatres
the snow flake
shattered like glass
to modesty in murder
the dread in the mind of the boxer
faced with razor-toothed
camera-snap
& to the truth
impossible to locate

i pray
for a response
to temptation
to the evils
in the bloodstream
the perils of knowledge

to 1969
& the magnitude of infinitude
to lifeless rivers of
maroon & crimson
to my own creations
however insignificant
the silhouette in the fog
constellations on a hot august night
the religions of the world
&
unbearable periods
of eruptive
silence

so long, troubadour

for Leonard Cohen (1934-2016)

there is no light
shining
through the cracks
in anything
today

only
the faint sigh
of that introspective gravel
lodged inside
my conscience

such a rare thing

   i recall
streaks
of silver-white light from
   the winter morning sun
pouring through
   the blind like elderflower wine
striping your face etched
in sleep
   peacefully
      content

that's how i remember you

calm   motionless
the subtle rise & fall
of your chest in
   time with timid white
      breakers
      lapping the edge of
         dry land

   like
   the only survivor on a
paradise island   morning after
   the great storm

you lie dancing through imaginings
hanging onto daylight
waiting to unravel dreams on
glassy sands
waiting for that salty touch of
these lips upon
yours

years later
as i struggle to recall your voice
i can't help but wonder if
you remember me
where you are
& if
those streaks of naked splintered ghost-light
illuminating that haunting beautiful
scar under your brow all
those years ago
have left any mark
at all

former

she disappeared to
          County Armagh
or Derry
or Belfast
or Morocco maybe

i don’t recall

postcards
hand written

what she was doing
who she was with
how much she wished things had
          been different

one day
they stopped coming

for
6
years
i kept them in a shoebox at
the back of the airing cupboard for
                    safekeeping

until one morning
in spring
          i guess

i took them into the garden &
buried them next
            to old Jake
fists clenched
blood
red

late night jazz

…in the absolute
        sifting

ivory tinkle with sad sax
painting the night

smoke cloud café
stale nicotine liberation

            a rush of stillness

late…

gin steamed
feet entranced by high-hat
            rattle
slide bass
            frag   menting
                  time

sky detonates sunrise

jazz robots -
            burning-muscular
receptive

beat-stricken
wonders

inviting
my
mind’s
eye
way past the metropolis

the gallows

i see
something
in
your eyes
that
words
cannot define
&
i know
as the poets
of
the
world
squeeze
their brains
dry
that i
must break
you
gently

i danced with you

after dark
upon
sodden fields

two lives
          one love

wired

to follow

she didn't see or hear it coming
& the letter fell helpless
in the muddied gutter
          postmarked Cornwall -
an apology to her Mum since she'd been
          a real bitch over christmas

Mum meant well
as most do
but she went on & on at times
          unnecessarily

the old fella at the roadside rushed to
          her aid
his hip ruined from overwork
& the driver screamed
piercing another late-september dusk

still the postman hurried along
sack on back -
a mad blind rush to meet
                    the final collection

that day on the seafront

i saw you today
walking along the harbour hand-in-hand
with another man

your secret life blown wide open
tripwire in my heart ready to go
blood frozen stiff
questioning everything

but still the waves tumbled in
the mountainsides reflected gold
seagulls sang to witches in the pinewoods
& children laughed at the world
as minutes turned into
years

& yet the ice-cream looked good
cheap too
dripping white
toffee shavings

the bench by the sand with
room for
one

MUM

from a son to his Mother

[2013]

i know

Mother

i know that you're tired

you have poured
blood & guts & bone
& soul
into my being
since i was a child

maybe now
you have nothing
          left

let it be

Mother

sometimes you try
& fix me
          when i'm not even
          broken

can you?

Mother

can you see the sun
like
i can?

pure love on the horizon
like
the faint chance
of
a smile
at the corners
of
your mouth

creation

Mother

at times when you look
at me
i see wonder in your eyes

the
sort
that
God must have had
when He carved
the
mountains out of
stone

transformation

Mother

your light burns
within me

i
am
learning
not to let
the darkness in

growing into something now

Mother

i feel the eyes of
many as they study every
inch
    of me

stroke
my jawline with
their
fingertips

seduce me with
something less than love

            i am no longer
                        a boy

Mother

i am

            a man

feeling words

Mother

i have to
write
my words down
because
          sometimes
when i speak
they
just
won't come

passage

Mother

as i was flying
far
above the continents
today
            i recalled hours
earlier
the crack in your voice
scraping away tears
as you bid me
farewell
again

i beg you
not
to cry when
i leave

instead
smile for the
opportunities
that you
have given
me

at the end of the day

Mother

my friend told me
that the poetry
i write
about you
is
beautiful

i
told her
        this is
        not poetry

this is
    the truth

testimony

[2014-2016]

sometimes

i
want to
climb out of my
bones
&
rest
for just a minute
in the
shadows
of my days

guilt

you gave me your heart
in a brown
          paper bag

told me
to
keep it safe
forever

instead
i smashed it
to
smithereens

trampled it
like
a
feral elephant

crushed it
as
though
i
were a

s
a
t
e
l
l
i
t
e

plummeting to earth

i deserve
nothing
from you but the worst
    of you
& yet
all you ever
bring
this
fallen man
    is love

Shakespeare wrote the most notable tragi-comedy

scaling the city streets of
Hong Kong
for
cheap beer
        at dusk

wading
through the rancid stench of
        grilled tofu
i plough on
masked // desensitised
hardened fog-drowned vendors
overworked &
        down on their luck

hey…sir…come in!

no!
i remonstrate with
the girls in
        dark doorways
hustling headlong toward dying lights
the immovable mass of
        blank faces
sliced fleshlong by fine rain

come on sir! come on!

i shudder
manic
time a weird sticky mess
&
stand up to
my full height
teetering
staggering
gripping the edges of sanity

stumbling
along soaked streets
burning wicked looks from passers-by
clawing at pores
they just know
clinking & clanking
feet in puddles

the heaviest of tip-toes
through steaming
rat-shit dreams

don't be surprised

if
i disappoint
you

it's the only
thing
i
know

dreamcatcher

she has eyes
like
troubled dreams
&
i hang
on the walls
grasping
          at something
anything
          everything
                    nothing

the dog
sleeps through it
          all

requiem for the lovers

i've grown because of what
          you did *to* me

not what you did *for* me

                    you say

          me
so near & yet so far
          preparing my latest
devastation
with the calmness
of a warm
dusk

you

remind me of the way
love should be

*

show me
what it is that really
matters

*

mean something new
every time
our eyes meet

*

take my breath
away
as
though
it's yours
to take

departure

i don’t hold you
to stop
you leaving

i hold you
so
you can guide me
wherever
you go

return of the muse

my pen
exploded on the
harbours of Hong Kong

one-hundred
floors
of fierce steel
peering
          down at me

untamed glorious sunbeams
          from
               above

shall i do it anyway?

the
poetry
i really *want* to write
i cannot
write

i
fear
that one day
you
might read it

call it wonder

i am
enchanted
by the aluminium
                    white dove
          that takes me
to places
i never
thought i'd see

aftermath

i am the bear post-hibernation
i am the ballad leaking thunder
i am the cockroach in its swarming
        cesspool heaven
i am the shark devoid of motive
i am the ghost in the machine
i am the story-teller without a voice
i am the pornstar
                balls deep
i am the vengeance in a million grins
i am the shocked emoji
i am the poet
        hidden within the melodrama

                so i am

b-sides

[1999-2017]

sabbath day

they shot me once
as the clock
        struck 3pm

shadows twisting in the square
where my brother fell
        a week earlier

the late-spring sun
a deepening shade of yam
screeching through
my eyes

i slumped heavy against the ruins
thick gloop & clots & bile leaking through
        my fingers into
citadels of sodden leaves bowed
at the edges like brain
skittered on cobblestones in
        tunnelled whips of wind

the burning street was
otherwise clean
scrubbed by drudges who swore
that bloodstains

were the art of the devil

my Brother’s neural tissue festering
blasted chunks & dented crucifix
          in a bucket somewhere
near the convent walls

a car hustled past
tyres shrieking // sirens
a Father wailing for his son

every year someone has to pay

i kept thinking of
my Mother’s last words

                    nothing is ever quite enough

kids were playing
kick-the-can around
          a maggot-ridden stray towards
                    the barracks

          i wanted to tell them
they shouldn’t be there
shouldn’t be witness
          to this

they laughed & cursed
their fading sound
        echoing through tight
        blistering alleys

the metallic clank of
        a crushed metal can
is no soundtrack
for death

i lived long enough to hear
the captors tamed by
the surge of an AA-52
whistling through bone so clean
it rang in my ears for
        the minutes i was spared

kids screamed & ducked
                into the cemetery
a women howled from a
        balcony
& i could smell gooseberries & shit
        spilling from my gut

it was sunday
i think

or maybe it wasn't

reasons for sharing

then the drums begin in the square
horns // merriment

          i look around for someone to
smile at // with   there is nobody
                    amongst everybody

children dance // rosaries
                    crowds applauding
          imagining futures

the last bus home // crowded // happy
nobody has text me today
                    not even once

& i realise
          why one whole
really is two parts
           of something no artist
could ever really
do justice

provincial town taxi rank

They came out the shadows of a side street through swathes of abandoned chip wrappers, dog shit and used condoms. The luminous glow from their phones glittered in the dusk. You could see their mean, affected scowls under tightly pulled hoods. The dark shadows of adolescence threatening to break through curled top lips.

The leader - a boy of probably eighteen - was tall and wiry with slouched shoulders and a twisted pout. His left eyebrow was part shaved, and his right hand looked like it was clutching something deep in his pocket.

The other three, swaggering in step, dipping first their right shoulders and dragging through with their left, were equally feral and of similar age. The one at the back, chubbier than the rest with fingerless gloves, wore a scarf that covered all but his eyes. He seemed to grunt with every step, as though preparing for war.

'What do we do?' Alice whispered, gripping my hand like the bars on a rollercoaster.

'Nothing. Just relax,' I said through clenched teeth.

There was still music from distant late bars falling idle onto empty streets - the last of the evening's revellers either long gone or locked in for the complete duration. There were still no taxis at the rank, and hadn't been for nearly twenty minutes.

Late December had turned bitter cold, a light blanket of ice starting to freeze on the windscreens of parked cars. The remains of a half-eaten donner kebab were slowly crystallising in the gutter; strips of pitta looking like aged oak.

'Spare us a cig there?' the leader growled.

'Ignore them,' I mouthed. Alice's eyes seemed to dilate, change.

'You listening to me, lad, or *what*?'

He strode into our personal space and Alice sunk into my side.

'We don't smoke.'

They laughed. The fat lad pulled out a lighter, passed it to the leader.

'You hear that, boys? They don't smoke.'

More laughter.

The leader's right hand never moved from his pocket as his left reached behind his ear and pulled out a cigarette, before tipping it into his mouth.

'You know how this works?' he snarled, flashing the lighter in front of my face. He did it half a dozen times. I had no choice but to back up.

'What is this?' I said, Alice tugging at my arm.

They laughed again. A well-oiled machine knows what to do when the situation demands it.

A glassy mist was descending on the rank, and there was no sign of headlights in the distance. Fear was confusing the words forming in my brain. The dull ache of premature sobriety started pumping through my temples.

'What *is* this!' one of the smaller boys mimicked in some sort of pre-pubescent screech, prompting more exaggerated laughter. The leader was close enough for me to smell the stale vodka and cannabis on his breath. His right eye was bloodshot.

'We're waiting for our lift,' Alice said suddenly, calmly. She seemed to straighten up and released her grip on my arm. The leader changed focus, staring down at Alice with a numb, threatening glare.

'Oh, sweetie,' he mocked, 'there is no lift. Not tonight.'

The tops of the buildings, mainly Tudor in style and construction, started to lean in, pressing on the streets below. The laddered sparkle from Christmas lights shimmered in successive strobic moments; carrot golds and nickels and charcoal blacks rattling in the space between the road and the horizon. The illusion of voices swept through the alleyways, a distant choir amongst ruins.

'That's enough,' I steadied, facing the leader head-on.

I'm a reader, myself. So is Alice. We spend nights on the sofa creasing the spines of a thousand books, curled up in one another's arms. Lost in different worlds. It's cliché to say that, at times, silence feels like a hurricane; we've both read it a million times and cringed. But my brain. Something murmured, then roared, then crashed into the back of my eyes like a tidal wave, splashing the night with violent shades of a certain kind of darkness I wasn't used to.

'The fuck you think you talking to?' he spat.

'You talking to 'im?' one of the others snarled, slapping the leader on the right shoulder. The fat boy stepped closer too, filling in the space on the leader's left flank, and for a split second they looked like compositions in the sketch pad of someone's nightmare.

'They're talking to me,' the leader mocked, pointing at his sternum.

'They're talking to you,' fat boy confirmed.

The leader faked a lunge; instinct saw me press him firmly in the chest, pushing him off balance. He seemed to crawl out of his slouch and stood up, full height, casually slipping out a blade from his right pocket.

'Boys,' he whispered, and it gave me the chills. 'I think this prick wants to dance.'

The fat kid leant awkwardly to the side, plucking something from within his shoe, his eyes wild with anticipation. Alice gasped and it sparked something in the smallest boy, who grabbed at the leader from behind, ushering him to stop.

'Come 'ed, Jay lad, let's get off.'

The leader swiped his arm away and turned back to face us. The knife was six inches long with a serrated edge. The fat kid had a flick knife; smaller but just as intimidating, flaming in the dull moonlight.

'Don't be so fucking stupid,' I said. 'There's cameras 'round here. We don't want trouble.'

'It's not about what *you* want,' the leader snarled, jabbing the blade at my chest. Alice started pulling me back, but the gang kept advancing.

'Stop!' she screamed. The echo rebounded in the distance.

'Get your fucking money and phones out and put them on there.' The leader nodded towards the street bin, and the fat kid started to circle us.

'Listen, there's no need . . .'

'Fucking do it!' he shrieked, his voice quivering.

I reached into my pocket, calmly pulling out my wallet and brand new iPhone X. *Little fucking bastard.* Alice had bought it as my Christmas gift, knowing business relied on it. I placed it on the bin and stepped back again.

'And your bitch, too,' the fat kid smirked, his shark-like, crooked teeth thumping on my retinas like rows of twisted gravestones.

'Don't call her that,' I barked, pointing at the fat kid. The leader jabbed at me, drawing blood.

'You fucker!' I cried, clutching at my hand. The leader stepped back.

'Let's go,' the small boy ached, backing up.

'Get the cash, let's go,' the other one agreed, but the fat kid smelt blood. He started lunging at us, side stepping, breathing heavily through his mouth and garbling something indecipherable. Alice threw her purse and phone onto the floor, and the fat kid snatched them up. The leader calmly took my wallet and phone off the top of the bin. The two smaller kids started to run, and the fat kid was sliding out of shot towards the alley.

Alice couldn't hold it in; she burst into tears, her face hidden in her hands. The leader backed up slowly, never taking his eyes off mine. Before he turned to run he flipped me his middle finger.

'Better get that checked, pal,' he mocked. 'Might get AIDS.'

rest home

screams unnatural to me
Mother looking down

ignore it // don't acknowledge it kind of scowl
so we shifted through
corridors
past rooms where skeletons with a lick
of skin rocked back & forth
unknowingly

past flowers aching in their vases
battling the air

the nurse with insomnia disguised
as black saturn rings
prised a smile from somewhere deep
walked us through the living room
where frayed suede armchairs swallowed
fading forms

accountants // doctors //
politicians // professors
lights out in eyes that once
saw vividly

a singer in the corner
they enjoy it the nurse lies

why do you miss when my baby …

nobody claps
TV's whip the walls with colour
comfort in an empty room
full of inevitabilities

she smiles time after time
holds my hand
hers almost dust in my palm
one last squeeze

she knows

the carpark is rammed i point at the singer
stealing a fag in the fine rains of september

don't point Mother berates *it's rude*

why didn't anybody tell me?

they told me all sorts of things

why Romeo wanted
Juliet so bad

manners

          the number of planets circling
the sun // the contracted
                    expression of pi

the colours on flags
          but never about borders

how to shoot basketballs // draw straight
cross streets without becoming death

as i got older they showed me how to
fill in forms // gel my hair
                    take a train // sing as though
                                        no-one was
                              listening
call the shots // read Winston Churchill
                    build a website // strike a match
          knock ten bells out of nails & cranks

say grace // drive a car // use condoms
never give in

they taught me how to lie

they kept telling me things
but nobody told me about this

left alone in rooms
towns & cities full of
bodies // faces
hollow promises

to figure that out
i needed a blackboard
a clock ticking like grenades falling
someone drenched in
suede & cotton pointing
at me // revealing me
organising & ordering me into
manageable incantations

i needed lists to be made
plans to be laid // a label to hang on my
head like a lampshade

i needed something that they never gave

now for forever

i banished you from
my head
though it made me sick to think of all
the hours i'd surrounded
you with arms &
promises of something
more than everyday
life

there were times
when forever
was nothing more than
cuddles through
movies as
cold nights moved
into town

sitting on park benches
at dusk
with insects &
the breeze

hot chocolate smiles
comfort in sadness

now
forever is today
        this afternoon
this hour
        this minute
                every glorious shitty second
        drifting through luck

the past close behind   fading
      tangled up
                wiry

morning before the flight home

breath in the last pipes failed
& the drunks
          in coastal dives finally
          called it a night   the last song sung blue
                    Neil Diamond
arms around shoulders of
      strangers
crackle & rattle of
          iced scotch in crystal

the streets
cool & sedate
tiny rollers skirting the
                sand with frothy
       white whispers

the way you smile
at me
when you're drunk
          feels like immortality

sand
between our toes
          sticky // cotton soft   complete release

mid-morning breakfast
wholesome sausage
egg // beans // suet // toast

the news big screens carved
into illuminated optics

Prince found dead at 57 . . .

beach breezes massaging
sun-kissed cheeks

no age . . . you whisper

time

don't ever forget about
the ones who
          crawl into gaps
                    waiting for something
          like a storm

the ones that
surrender
when bullies take their
                    lunch money

the ones
whose sadness
paints pictures with something
        less than colour

don't ever walk
the streets
presuming everyone has
                    somewhere to go
              like you

that
the ever decreasing
minutes

are filled with anything
                    more than nothing

or
that time

                    that little bastard
with plastic fingers

          holds anything
          but
endings
for
those desperate
for
new
beginnings

village supermarket in january

precincts below my window
lush with fresh-fall

horizons
absent within vast vapours of
electric white

i follow the ascent of my breath
curling // twisting into
mist as running engines
claw
at compact frost

relieved gasps
tumbling through sliding doors
wrapped up
like onions –
bobble hats & snoods & ski-gloves
wind-burnt glowing cheeks // noses
knowing smiles between strangers

it's winter
& it's edgy

…but fun

we really shouldn't have bothered in this
somebody mutters
without meaning it

the floor a darkening mass of sludge

navy blue uniforms arc the isles with
virgin mops warning
old folk – tread with care

where has the sky gone?
squeaks the little girl
in the supermarket
queue

the snow is giving it a rest
her Mother smiles

first at her then at me

so many questions

who knows
how
8am
turns into
6pm

the years
turn into aches
& pains

how children
grow
so far
from dreams

who knows
where
rainbows go
when all
is said
          & done

where
      lullabies
are sung

where
night owls
hoot

where
smoke
in
the chimney
f
l
o
w
s

who knows?

we are made of

cells
that bind us

that glue
blood // muscle // bone

the space
within spirits

dark
webs of
stars

burning worlds

you are punctuated by

tenderness
home & bone
longing
jazz
odd juxtapositions
menace
sparrow song & violence
Samuel Beckett
an inability to forget
smug de-facto critics
that raging glorious monsoon voice in
          movie backdrop cities
poets &
          cheap talk
flashbulb adoration & lust
fat & flesh
music
whispered trees
clock faces halted // reborn
knots of apple greens across marmalade skies
pieces of man scattered
          on undiscovered shorelines
scalpels over words on pages
heart-wrenching
          beautiful vignettes

death under railway arches
in the summertime
faux nostalgia
fear
bodies tied up in car boots
in dreams
dancing girls
cocks bulging in silky trunks
disco disco disco
needles down back passages
the dead salute
slide guitar & Soho nights
the old guy that should've been a star
encounters in cubicles
spider bites in foreign lands
Boracay
snapshots of mountain men
alcoves in worn-out pubs &
faces already dead waiting
to die
Sheppard's *Twentieth Century Blues*
subways & alleyways in deprived
seaside towns
towers falling in nations
impenetrable
little wings heading for the sun
ocean scenes
naked hot spring carelessness

morbid news stories
square-eyed numb cinema freaks
liars in power
cheats in the box-seats
£'s & $'s
tragedies on K2
the last night of the earth &
        bazaars loaded with possibilities
open veins & minds & doors
hummingbirds defeated
Sleaford Mods
        magic realism
my diary underneath the tree which
                said all the things you'd
                    longed never to
                        hear
bubbling jacuzzis in winter
the race to the summit
drainpipe jeans on *Top Of The Pops*
stale pipe smoke &
        sausage roll satiation
Speilberg's *Jaws*
vinyl spinning more than yarns
the hour striking 3am
storms upon Tryfan & cars
            abandoned in car parks
love at a distance
the fresh aroma of mint or lavender

accidents on motorways
fogged identities
livestock awaiting your plates
dancehall massacres &
                lowkey extremists
binge-watching drama
charity shop imaginings
booze 'til dawn
dirty looks on packed buses
dusty books
paranormal documentaries in
                                hotel rooms
magnetic iceberg charm
seasons without promise
skin-bruised bullseye infatuation
loving someone
          who could kill you
                    twice
well-dressed yuppie types in exclusive playgrounds
                                for the rich
vans carrying information
waterfalls of hair
vocals way back in the soup
postmodernists
zionists
reformed fascists
vertical images of long-forgotten heroes
Leon Trotsky

Rome burning // speechless
guardians without voices without eyes
banal art in
        concrete jungles
career hitmen
train tracks leading south again
every word ever spoken
shadow men waiting round the bend
        somewhere up ahead
                inside our tiny broken
        collective head
foetal rain & candle flares
city boy blues
the thought of George Mallory gripping
                        the North-Face for generations
churches & prisons on sundays
slippery knowledge
kidneys on the brink
nurses queuing at food banks
Attenborough's grave predictions for 2040
the birth of the non-servant
introspection
protests on promenades
Frank O'Hara's rusty pen
plastic in the bellies of mutants
wheelchairs hurtling
                toward glass
two-a-penny smiles

when you most expect it
the bitter battle-axe in supermarket aisles
rattling bolts on rollercoasters
hand-woven linen
the complete history of barely anything
street vendors in gutters
Wrestlemania
the Lizard-King & the toxic
short-lived American dream
business expenses in strip clubs
[mdma] ●●
whimpers in street grids
poltergeists & the seven devils
biological Fathers
just faces in photo albums
bodies suspended in chamaecyparis obtusa in
Aokigahara Forest
the announcement of DNA in The Eagle
spicy bubbling Cantonese
broth
soft white underbelly transfiction
christmas trees in january
pronouns in the 21st century
9/11
flame // smoke // (last) moments
Elvis dead
the bullied kid who fights back
arbitration in junkie town

recreation on tired weeknights
747's lapping globes
lapping shores
lapping olympic tracks laden with records
lapping it all up whilst we can
botanists of styles
fighting tooth & nail for
the beaches
reality TV aftermath
Viking raids on Lindisfarne
full stadium claustrophobic hell
yoga in basements in
far away places
adrenaline shots when veins open up
stark & simple illustrations
sacrifices
revolutions
Bibles burning in bins
& lifeblood tears
learning to avoid problems rather than solve them
fireworks in libraries
Scousers making waves &
dire straits in mining towns
misery & resolution
Chaucer // Shakespeare // Gabriel García Márquez
brides walking ailes alone
the witness behind the stone
alley-cats with swagger

iconic album covers hung in museums
senseless comics
size 26 in the dressing room
armed borders
bird eating goliath spiders in
                        late-night doorways

teachers who know nothing
loyalty in all the wrong places
segues into
            parallel worlds &
                        the devastatingly
            underrated
        grief
      at
losing dogs

snap-shot

We were just kids being kids. That's all.

Long hot summers playing down by the river, wasting time, fantasising. There were four of us in those days.

All I ever wanted to be when I was ten years old was a champion swimmer. You know, stood in front of a crowd with my medals held high. Honoured, confident, fit. Big muscles and an even bigger smile. Family looking on with pride, friends looking on with envy. That was the pinnacle of my dreams. Life is simple when you're ten.

I *loved* to swim.

But when the river was high I never swam. Folks in the village told tales about kids going missing in the summer drifts. How river monsters had taken them. It rained a lot in the summers, you see. Monsoon rains at times; the type you can barely see through or breathe in if you stand there too long. The sort of rains I used to stare at in wonder through the porch windows of the farmhouse.

Where did it come from?

It was enough to blow the mind of a kid like me. I was a good swimmer, but I wasn't too smart. Teachers said I couldn't concentrate for long. Always dreaming and imagining, and doodling in the corners of my jotter.

One day, I drew a river monster and the teacher snatched my pad off the desk.

The rainy season here can be pretty fraught. The pathway down through the woods to the riverbank was always flooded after heavy rain, and we had to wear our wellies or we'd never make it through the sludge and mire. The river was wide and very beautiful to me, splitting several valleys and running down to the canyon. It was a very famous river, Mother had told me. She said I should be grateful to live in the palm of Mother Nature. I didn't know who Mother Nature was, but she sounded nice enough.

The village folk were quiet and went about their business. Most people had their jobs to do, especially the old folk, who always seemed to be pottering around with tools and instruments in their gardens and the village square. Occasionally one would disappear - the old folk that is. Mother said they'd been taken back to heaven to be cared for by the Lord. Very few ever came to the riverbank though. It held bad memories for some of them, Mother said, but I didn't know what she meant. River monsters only came when the river was high, they said. When the river is high, stay on the banks, they said. They grab kids playing close to the rapids by the ankles and drag them to their deaths, they said.

That's what happened one Friday in 1992.

His name was Robert, but we called him Bob. He was a chubby kid. Always seemed to be eating something. Was as clumsy as hell. Candy, ice-cream, skewers of barbecued marshmallow, potato chips and popcorn. My Mother said shame on his Mother for letting him get that way, but I didn't understand what she meant.

Bob was always happy and laughing with the other kids. His milk bottle glasses with one taped arm are still etched in my mind. It's the one defining thing about Bob that has never left me in all these years.

Years erase the important things, don't they?

First it's someone's mannerisms, then it's their voice, then it's their face. Sooner or later you're only left with a name.

He was my friend, was Bob.

Bob was just Bob.

When it happened I was sitting on the bank playing with my tape player. It was brand new – a birthday present from Mother. I knew she'd worked her guts out to buy it. Had a copy of The Beatles *Rubber Soul* inside when I unwrapped the brown paper. I'd had it on repeat ever since. You'll cost me our home in batteries, she'd said one day looking annoyed, but I didn't understand what she meant. I loved that song about a yellow submarine. I could just see that place in my dreams, especially after a long day playing in the heat.

It was such a serene afternoon. There was no breeze, and the sun was so strong that everything in the distance shimmered like the reflection from a prism. Like someone was holding my eyes and shaking them really fast. In the distance we could hear the rumble of a mower cutting chess boards into turf, and every now and then barking from the sheepdogs on a neighbouring farm. Everything seemed so perfect, and I could feel myself growing sleepy as the late-afternoon quilt of unshaded warmth draped itself over our lives.

Then something happened pretty quick.

I felt it and then I saw it.

At first he lost his balance a little. The rapids had been flowing pretty fast, and Bob had stumbled out a little far towards the drift. Way further than we were ever allowed to go, even when the river was low. By the time I'd looked up he was struggling with his balance. Then, in what seemed like forever, our eyes met and his laughter turned to terror. That moment went on for years. Decades. A lifetime.

I could see the dimples in his cheeks, the ends of his curly hair wet with sweat, and his thick eye-brows contorted around helpless eyes.

Then he was gone.

The eulogy was read by Father Stevens, who was Roman Catholic and loved a drink. I saw him slip himself a whiskey from a hip flask later that day. He was stood by the buffet sandwiches at the wake and didn't think anyone was watching. I was watching. He had a purple nose with protruding veins, and silver hair that reflected the sun. I'd witness his own eulogy years later, in front of the biggest congregation our village had ever seen.

Mother said the eulogy Father Stevens delivered about Bob was beautiful. Captured Bob perfectly. I hadn't listened too closely. I was fixed on Bob's Mother, hysterical, who was being held up by some other tearful ladies I'd never seen before. The front pulpit was so loud.

They brought a coffin, but I don't think he was in it. No, I definitely don't think he was in it, but I never asked. I just looked at Mother, and she at me, and knew I'd never swim again.

bandages

i’m sick of smiling when it makes me weak
i’m sick of trying when the days
amount to this
i’m sick of silence flooding my ears &
weighing me down

i’m sick of doctors fixing their ties
as they tell me
bad news

i’m sick of seeing my Mum’s face turn numb when
she’s sees me lying there
alone the other kids outside
in the sun

i’m sick of having answers but
never knowing the questions

i’m sick of being sick
which is rich because if i wasn’t
i’d be out in the sun
& these poems
would never
get done

i woke up thinking i was Miles Davis

the world will be better for this
        they said

covered in scars & Mick Jagger jowls
        i couldn't make love
so i left the bedrooms of
the world
put myself on stages where
        lasers hid the burning-ready
salivating red-eye of
    voyeurs needing blood

we sat beside windows in twos
        post-show
blind to the unfamiliarity of
the sounds outside

they will open their ears
        they said

tender as a habit
i motioned for the door
which wasn't quite open
wasn't quite shut
afraid of something less than hush

ready for seaweed
ready for pelicans in cages
the ghosts on the stairs
fish choking
          on fresh air

they need to go home now
          they said

the lights went down

                    the show was over

(de)generation

the heavens unbolted
& so it seemed odd
that you . . .

yet we made it

what is this that
makes me
righteous? you take a small part
of you & fix me

patch me up like a nurse
pretend that i'm at least
part of something
whole

it was only in primark months later
watching conformity
explode
i realised
i was the chapter
i hadn't written

it was *me*

my culminations
on repeat
spray-painted on your eyes
every time
you smiled

which reminds me
something fatalistic i guess i understood

you sank soothingly into
level -1

consort

the night
        black as panic

you wave at me
through the eastern edge of Spain
into Morocco   the coastal medinas of Algeria
        gazing out at Mediterranean dusks

we reconvene in Tunisia
        where you hand over inscriptions
                        engraved in bone
i hand them back without a word   we board
        a boat to Sicily // ride the trains through Italy

you watch me like a woman
            cabin lights flickering
we part at the port of home
like blackbirds scattering
                into unripe dawns

the memory of your 4×4   the black tunnel

                you never once look back

vacation

here we are
dipping toes in the lagoon
unshaded from the temple of
the sun
the echoes of
a distant city riding on
waves // crashing against
silken rocks

we are far away your eyes suggest
from the world of cholera &
bank accounts // car crashes
breaking news
school dinners // accident & emergency rooms
fish bones
silent drones
cold war at the kitchen table

we are farther from our roots
than we've ever been
yet
closer to home
than we've ever known

in cities

& come to think of it
we saw the vicar
stumbling down Hope Street with
          knickers dangling
from his suit

the headmaster
in the bookies scoffing cookies on
          his lunch hour // screaming at screens
                    "you fuckin' beaut!"

the cleaner in
marigolds applying lippy
                    in car windows

"never speak to strangers!"
       shouts the purple-nosed drunk
               propped up by his
lollipop // halting drug-money vans
                              outside the Cabbage Inn

& the rain is pounding the wheelie bins
as drenched uniforms scamper through
puddles to the bus where
                    pensioners scowl

"ain't nowt' to lose when you're full of booze!"
warbles the man slumped // shoulderless in
the disabled seat

& i couldn't help but part-agree
since who was the fool?

him? or *me*?

'you' is not reserved for two

winter covered the islands
with low mist
gripping my ankles

a small matter of
the excitement you gave me

messages flooding my phone
(howls of anguish from home)
watching you laying out the loungers through palms
skin a deep oily brown
eyes reflecting the ocean

& i see two faces the face i've come to know
& the face that i crave

gently riding the waves to
shore // stirring something
unwanted within me

it was evening when
we first met
you - stood by the open fire in
that bookshop

staring into
space as the poet read aloud

& i’ve always thought since
that you were
dreaming of me that night when
his words tumbled down
like paragons

you, more beautiful than any crashing wave
or dissolving sunset

or any palm leaf shading me from
certain sins

the old man

seagulls take flight
with scraps of
            our lives

& there's a man
who's been out sailing
                    smelling of salt air
sucking on scotch in
harbour vaults
watching the horizon fall
like ancient civilisations

the last of
the day's waves
creeping apologetically over
          settled shells

          while we're all so busy
                    being free

for the purpose of experiment

gather prized possessions
skulk towards windows
toss them onto streets
                    heavy with voices

run wild-eyed down hollow stairs
can of petrol in hand
          dance around the heap

douse it   douse it   douse it

strike a match & freeze the scene

lie amongst cinders
          eyes like spinning plates

wait for howls of black alarms

everything
          in its right place

secret

i held you in my hand
like a Russian doll
excavating layer by layer
riding the curves with
                    my forefinger
the sac below my penis
      aching heavy
bruises bending down my veins
your eyes flirting with the tenderness
                    of my throat

i have lived
& you have lived
          but this is living

late october

the clocks go back tonight

i'll watch those hands
go round & round 'til midnight comes
take us all back to yesterday
with a simple twist
                    of plastic

there'll be no knocks at my hunk of pine
no rattles at my venetian blinds
no tapping at the window panes
or vibrations on my phone again
          & again & again

               nothing but
       the night   & like old lovers
unfolding   relapsing   remoulding
     the crescent midnight moon
            enthroned
                  high above the rain

craving

your eyes
open up before me
like doors
to something possible

why

do
you make something
that should
        feel like love
    hurt
        like war?

stretched across vast continents
my iPhone vibrates
            as cities rock back & forth
like babies
in the palms
            of mountain ranges

isn't it time

the first to rise on
a sunday morning
i gather my thoughts
in no particular order

stroll ankle deep
down beaches
watching soft swells chase the shoreline
then retreat with something
like regret

your email
won't leave me be…

…isn't it time you
came back home?

i walk past
bars i
have little recollection of

the swollen lips i've kissed
eyes belonging
to those worth more
than sex

it’s all trickling back
through
those cracks between
escape & truth

    i
return to the hostel
partiers beginning to rise
                    all tatty-headed
          swollen-eyed
                    fog-breathed

things on their mind
that can wait
          ’til tomorrow

one night in Phuket

your eyes
the colour of sand & sea

i looked
into your world
        for lifetimes within hours

i sacrificed my walls
        to complete you

opened
you up like doors to
            another world

held myself   breathless
        deep inside your skin
                as the bass shook layers
                    beneath us

walked the sands
        long after midnight

        hands entwined…

                    …our way of letting go

lights
on the harbour
    ringing in my brain

i slept through the alarm
& you were gone

another crowded minivan
cramped
with filthy souls
    & wandering laundry

heading for anything

    more
        or less

oasis

on winter afternoons
the sea   your eyes
towns imploding
          nothing seems to add up

                    implicitly
we take turns   undressing
        these words mean . . .
the waves ending in fizz & lather
i move within you // without you
cry ourselves to sleep –
          we just don't understand
                              love

alone in an attic room   weeks later
wind punching at the skylight
          i'm drunk a lot
sick days at the office // only lamplight

the earth still spinning   that's physics
            & you are somewhere
    co-ordinates   the axis revolving

i stand in the kitchen   naked
          sing for the joy of it all

35

[2018]

fantasy

maybe
the only time
i
really
love you
is when
i
am between your legs

maybe
the only time
you
really
love me
is when
          i'm gone

nobody ever really knows

maybe a terrible aching death
        awaits me

maybe i will die in my sleep
        aged 93

maybe the stars will implode
& catapult us all
        toward serenity

maybe the trash collectors of the world
        will blow up wall street

maybe Paul McCartney will
        live forever

maybe you will fall &
            split this thin ice of modern life

maybe i will pick you up
                or maybe i won't

maybe a colony of Bigfoot will emerge
from the pages of cryptozoology & shake
                the foundations

maybe we will scream until
        silence reigns

maybe the losers
will come through & win

maybe we will start again
primitive cool
        // pure survival

maybe i will drink this tea
        steaming green
hibiscus tint
before it reaches lukewarm

maybe the insane greed that pours blood & bone
        into marble & stone
will surrender itself
hands aloft
        on every street

maybe we will rock'n'roll

maybe the wild-eyed-wanderers of the world
        will return home
to find that everything is nothing

        it was all just reverie

maybe the sweeping technological advances
that turn streets cold &
gather the masses into deep
insane pits of addiction will
spontaneously combust

maybe us & them
will just become us

maybe they will love
& i will love
& you will love
& love will
reign supreme

just

maybe

no use

i
tried to heal you
by
fucking you

but

fucking you
opened
wounds
you never knew
you had

a miracle

when i look at you
i think it's a miracle that
we were
put on earth in
the same space at
the same time

all the years
& decades
& centuries
that could have been chosen
for us

all the places
on this vast planet
that we might
have grown

all the billions of lives
entwined
that we have waded through
to touch skin

our lives
our time

our chromosomes
                    aligned

we sit
across tables
          across nations
across universes
          across smiles

two temporary skins
eternally bound

a miracle

religion

i am scared of dying

don't be

they say

you are only returning home

anti-religion

don't give yourself
to the heathens

they tell me

don't commit yourself
to their fantasy

you implore me

another night

over

& i'm walking home alone
again
midnight
long gone
streets deserted bar the occasional
drone of distant taxis
on
main roads
humming like wasps in summer
returning
the surrendered // hen-pecked // exhausted
to their cold
marital beds

no such (bad?) luck
for me

instead
the hiccup
of an overloaded gut &
the smog of uncertain
notions
repeating

in the cool late-night
gusts

needing voices // fearing voices
&
i've only got a t-shirt on
because a crowded pub is always warm
even in winter
the breath of a hundred husky voices
bouncing off walls
cheap talk &
expensive drama

the cunt at work
gym guy with new wheels
the player with the
fake tan
the price of being worth something
hot moms in school yards
the jock with the big cock
Trump & co.
George Michael dying
Prince dying
Bowie dying
Leon Russell & Guy Clark & George Martin &
Glenn Frey dying
seemingly *everyone* dying

& we can’t help
but remember the times
our Mothers would say
don’t go out without your coat or
you’ll regret it later on

or the times
our Fathers would say nothing
at all
unless they were told to

but i don’t need to i’d say
i’m only going to be in a taxi & then
straight in the bar

then that uncompromising stare

... put it on

in my mind
the streets on fire
& the madhouses & the brothels & the squats
& the nightclub side alleys
supermarket car parks
cemeteries // dormitories // taxi ranks
// junkyards
they’re all
up in flames

but
the parades are numb
tonight
every night
everywhere

& you look
curtains drawn
lights off
gates closed
eyes closed
rapid movements counting sheep
the occasional gang
fearing their own shadows
even the cats are quiet
they've fucked themselves
into oblivion
scratched their way
into a million
feline dreams

& it's like
all my urges have been switched on
at once
a warehouse of naughty
imaginings
suddenly drowned in light

but
the reality is worse than
the sum
of my fantasies // my unkissed
lips drowned in bad oil
the stench of fried chicken
lingering in my armpits
one of the last signs of the night
one of the first signs of
exquisite loneliness

the minutes
move faster than my feet
& i can feel dawn creeping up behind me
like halloween
another 4am
festering
with the world wide web
&
memories of a fading youth
spinning the wheel

round & round

& round

&
round

comeback

what is this shit?
you say
throwing
a pile of poems
at me
you found in the
drawer

what kind of man writes this shit?

the kind of man that lives with someone like you
i say

gathering up the papers
noticing
the clock
strike
6.15 am

someone to love

you lie
as naked as an x-ray
half
illuminated
by
the early morning sun

&
i wait
in the doorway
exploring the contours
of your back

7:32am

not even
            the tribulation
could break this
silence

in chains

i have wanderlust

i guess i need you to know

it's no use
keeping me under lock & key
putting blinkers on me
pulling me away when someone
new enters the
frame

i'll always break free
when you believe you have my
every limb
my every whim
my everything
in chains

i could say i'm sorry
but
then
i'd have to
mean it

voluntary exit

sometimes i think
how nice it would be to
get off this planet

post-ejaculation
watching breaking news
teenage balding
the inability to refuse

travelling on buses
sunday mornings coming down
Donald Trump – leader of the free world
this twisted
rat-race merry-go-round

American sitcoms
listening to blood-boiling canteen clitter-clatter
putrid drains & dog-shit stains
mars bars cooked in
heart-attack batter

Mothers-in-law
low-budget economy plane seating
minimum wage in
provincial towns

school bullies handing out a routine
beating

dentists // loan-sharks
terrorism // fundamentalism
standing room on
jam-packed subways
fallen angels
evangelism
Elvis dead at 42
the sickly smell of hospital sweat
homophobia // inscience
forever stuck in mounds of debt
cockroach slime
the k.k.k

circle jerking // supercilious smirking
never knowing what to say

cheese & onion wotsits
blowing up history
monks burning at the crossroads
insincere reverie

5.15am in winter
the horror of teeny-bop-pop
touring temples
for the sake of it

the diet that starts
        tomorrow because you just
                can't
                    stop

corned beef & crème caramel
        Brexit
cancer // Justin Bieber
bungee jump numbness on
                a gambling island
the realisation that you have
        to leave her

farts with no windows
homicide when
        walking the dog
the backstreets of Thailand at 11pm
grisly plane crash death of
                      rock & roll
when they should never have taken off
        in fog

                rap music
blackheads // cysts // right-wingers
nonces in the senate
extra-marital
        sticky fingers

napalm bombs
surrogate childhoods
doubting yourself
          before asking for a date
& strange noises at dusk
                    coming from the woods

extinction // body odour
cheating tuk-tuk taxi drivers
a hair in your food that
                    knocks you sick
massive bird-eating spiders
crack-house sex
genocide
          avocado shaped heads
serial killers offering anyone // everyone
                              a free ride

bum notes in a symphony
decapitation of one's epiphany
abandonment & social class systems
the futile
          never-ending quest
               to be free

green with envy
wikileaks
the iPhone four-hundred & fifty-seven

the tragic kid at school who reeks
snapped string in a searing solo
devils in my head
families skating on thin ice
chemical weapons &
        the living dead

soldiers coming home in boxes
Mothers crippled // slumped in arms
fat-cat politicians
    faking grief & remorse
twisted rhetoric
       false alarms

& then
the question nobody has
        time to consider:

    what if this idea
        of fake news
     really is just
        fake news?

she never got what she wanted

the captain disembarked
as i scratched at another
hunk of skin

you don't know that my dreams
have become tear-stained elephants
he said
you don't know that my retinas have become
my knees

the blood began slowly
coagulating as my
thoughts climbed all over
the captain like
tarantulas

this is the dead-pool!
he screamed
crammed into spaces in
his immediate
personal history

i watched my own birthday celebration
through the keyhole of a locked cupboard
he wept

the slowly growing
crowd of nobodies going
nowhere
touching up their eyes with
lemon-scented tissue

the captain took out
a picture

this is my
calendar girl
he said

i contemplated murder
since there was little
else to do
but i was
interrupted by the sound
of egg-shells under the
politically incorrect

i studied
the lines
on the forehead of
the face of
the calendar girl
& sighed

a deep melancholy
limped into
the stale sound above &
        below us

the captain began to chant
        without his
                usual air of reticence:

give us this day
        our daily bread
                . . . breaking into wail

the month was unbeknown to
        either of us
& i guess it
    hardly mattered

the passage of the centuries
        has taught us that cowardice
                        is genetic
                i suggested

        he rallied &
wiped severe humiliation
        from
            his senses

Janis came into
the room
        & the captain
unpeeled his face
        // handed it to her

i cannot give you my heart
the captain told her
                not even a piece

        ... *it has melted*
                into my veins

disintegration

[2019-2020]

images

wait until you see yourself
in spring lake
        reflections

in the luminous heavy looking glass

in spiralling winds on
                plains in april

as months shift
like blackbirds preparing broods
        in colour
you will see yourself in teardrops
      in autumnal mists
           over russet meadows

in spider-web-december snowflakes

in the first tomorrow
        you'll ever remember

dreamcave

the candlelight
at the back of the garden
somehow reminds me
          of you

i watch it burn deep
into dreams
dancing on the zephyr
to the tinkle of
          wind-chimes

watch fire
bleed & rise onto
     cold stone

take myself to bed

                    alone

lament

are these words
formed out of remembering?

memories
like bronze in an early winter sunset
clinging to trees

those things you said

words
climbing on me
like fingers over the
shoulder

a coin
in the wishing well
reflections in
weighty shimmering
silver

little kids
watching with expressions
way beyond their years

signs

the bullwhip
of voices in the hall
          woke us

light formations on diamond tiles

shadows under the door

the next day // blossom under branches
          faces in the woods
figures shifting

          shapes &
               rare imaginings

you said they were here
          & a part of me believed it

i didn't say goodbye
before i drove
          toward the coast

some people have no poetry

what do they *do*?

do they ever go
to see
storms stroke the heads
of apartment blocks?

what do they reach for
when winter raps the windows
in late november?

when he comes
through the door
huddled
in sheepskin // puts his
bags down
& smiles?

how do they look into
the eyes
of another
& see anything but
themselves?

sundown over shadowlands

i was left wondering if
        the sunlight
would ever make it through
                the keyhole

if i would ever hear voices again

if anybody
            sat in the pub on
                        saturday afternoons
in front of TV screens & horses
            would recall
                    my name

            our names

if the bus-stops in the villages
            even exist anymore
now that we roll towards something
                    entirely different
                then one
                    another

postcards from 1999

it's all a journey

a fear of losing

losing multiplies
            like numbers

careering into future moments
dragging the past
          under glowing wheels

          memories //
strobes in the pleasuredome

silence on
the streets at dawn
      watching headlights
            slog through rains

hauntings
      that we endure

chain

the daisy chain
hasn’t long broken

you sit beneath the crack willow
reading poems
by Maya Angelou

i’m fixing it
i grin
twisting them round
thumb & finger

fix it so it’ll never break
you whisper

firecrests

nibs of blood
plumed the edges of your
          fingernails

i held you –
so much gestured
so little understood

someday we won't know one another
you slurred
          almost inaudible

dressed in yellow you were in bloom

the slow melt of butterflies into
the nakedness of shadows
          into dirty blood-axe greens

birds captive in
sizzling sallow tulips
            calling into catkins

calling into

                    call   …ing

that time i just couldn't ask

through foam
our toes

gull-threaded surfs
curl around border lights

your hair
the flush of blood

you
moving through solid air & space
reserved for something still

waves gaining urgency

my questions hanging on
the edge

of

now

down the line

it's 4am

dawn climbs her infinite horizons

i am drunk // dishevelled
          amidst milky rising light

dawn chorus peeling
skin from under deepened eyes

i see it like a movie in
                    space & time

powder exploding

a terrible dream
          drowning in glory & fag ends

you ask me where i want to go

i say
wherever you are going

innards

you are the part of me
they cannot see
on scans

i've had it here
you say
though i can't believe it

the spice upon my upper lip
tremor down the backbone

fuck Brexit you laugh

packing bags
glowing fingernails
the rust upon my heart strings
in A-minor

there's more to be had
zipping seams like violence

motion in my retinas

the clock
about to strike the hour

headlines

the news said
the convoy had exploded
        across the river

the news said
the dead included teens
      not long enrolled

the news said the families had been
              informed & were in
                    'a bad place'

the news said nothing about us

              i called friends
told them i should have done this & that
should have said *i need you* more
walked with you in the mornings
        held you in the evenings

stopped myself when…

when the hearts of two poets break

they write all
the things
they hoped they'd
never have to

lie down
too much

ponder over playlists
that exacerbate pain

worship
the object
with irrational hope

embrace tragedy
like a
sad-eyed dog

message
each other
with encouragement that takes
all their
strength

as though
the buttons on their
cell phones
are lined with lead

hurl their hurt
at
computer screens
with
something
resembling
bravery

something resembling
fear

nothing
that is anything less
than truth

Belisama

[2021]

the bones of dogs

the bones of all my dogs
are in the dunes

all four of them
with one to follow

salt-water clean
& stripped of marrow

there won't be anymore after that

unless
        maybe
they bury me there too

gift for a lover

you were rubbing
the petals
of lush white chickweed
gently
between finger & thumb

just far enough away
not to intrude
the clink & clack of
the old
wooden roller coaster
anchoring
skytrails from
Woodvale air base

a silhouetted // derelict toad-hall
crooked on the headland

later
we entered the bookshop
a smell of musk
& jasmin
an old fireplace
ready for winter

they wrapped it
in brown paper
& you clutched my arm
grateful

when we reached the promenade
the kids were being packed away
claimed by dinner time &
               tired eyes

the drunk didn't notice as we passed
his bench
though i could have sworn
i saw him stir at
the crinkle of brown paper
when she pulled it out
glowing
    at the name

images of home & lifeboats

it rained on saturday
then it rained again on
          sunday
but i braved torrents on
the coastal path
wet socks // red-raw face
conscious of the years climbing
          over the sands
then retreating
     like the rough tide

the rig looked like a
delicate candle sat
on the horizon as though
          a shelf
the echoes
of tragedy lingering
in soft mists on
the water
& faded photographs
     in local pubs

     a gruff winter
i made it to
          the marshland
fantasising
about warm bubbles beside
spinning vinyl

maybe some
lemon & honey

        & a tired dog

the flat bare
        but never empty

smalltown boy

the marina
sheet-clean indigo surface
edges decorated with one rusted
kwiksave trolley from
the 80's
half in
// half out
under the
barricade
dressed in weeds &
dull plastic

this is where the ducks
sigh

this is where your Father grew up
this is where he
had a fight in school
this is where he learnt to give women
black eyes
this is where your Mum hid the empty bottles
this is where the boys robbed
tills in corner stores & newsagents
with tiny aisles

this is what you ran from

i *know* it is
& i felt for you

this is how you unlearn it all
          by coming back

walking far enough out
that quicksands might surround
                    you
          like those gangs did

                              out & out & out

trying to reach the horizon

ribble view

one strung buoy
          treading water
before a backdrop of stick-thin turbines
whipping dust off
Snowdonia

i peer out
thumbing a frayed watch strap
ears full with gloopy
ice-cream van
jingle
thinking *this isn't so bad*

helleborine

you stopped on the trail
the sea & sand like brushstrokes
          up ahead

i waited
as you waded into bracken
reaching for that soft
delight

years later
you told me angels
had clustered at
          the tall hillock
overlooking
sand-fogged valleys

&
i believed you

          it was just easier that way

bygone

the Irish sea
as grey as your sickly skin

images of cities
dissolving
fog rumbling in through
fine rains & mist

the geography
      of your spine;
the curvature
the gentle balance of the discs
the surrender of
            limp shoulders

everything now
that will soon be nothing
shingle crunching underfoot
            soft off-white

a kid storms out
      from the hall of
            mirrors // crazed
bellowing *but it's still early…*

we find a bench
& you study the plaque
            carefully

arcade

the confusion of music
feels psychotic

the smell of torched caramel
& frying fish turning my nose from a
vast ocean
          where a lone swimmer
navigates the morning
all alone
with his thoughts

olympia

leaving the discotheque
          at dawn

liquor frosted
          // alone

the hum of a solitary engine
navigating
splintered borders of
a motionless fairground

two girls
rag-bag // post-party
feeding swans

joint
   curling
towards 7am

cinematic

          unfiltered

the douglas complex

  they say
there are shipwrecks
sleeping on choppy sandbanks
somewhere out
  towards that rig

as a boy
i was convinced it
was a transformer
bounding towards the shore

then i grew
& my imaginings hardened
like leather shoes
in puddles

i can't look out there now
because it reminds me
of something
  i can no longer have

COVID-19
VACCINE

lockdown suburbia

[2020-2022]

day 1

somebody says *it's getting worrying this*
                    & faces curl

the bell
brings speculation

didn't someone eat a bat?

my chicken
          feels tough
the pasta sauce too salty

lessons to be learnt
          i think

day 3

flights grounded

panic mutating

where are the carriers?

shut the borders

somewhere i read
that this is the plague

predictions
incomprehensible numbers
(everyone's going to
lose someone)

eerie laughter & suspicion

this is state control

i'm not so sure…

start scrubbing my hands

forget about that coffee
with friends

lock the inside door
as well

day 6

home seems cosy

i prepare for the worst
scrub the surfaces
bleach pots & pans
scale door frames with disinfectant
turn Coltrane down
        that little bit quieter

i don't want people knowing i'm in

you mustn't have anyone round
Mum says in
        that voice

    turn on the news

volume muted

        the faces say it all

this
        is

                science

        fiction

day 8

it's taken
the famous musician on
        Merseyside

silenced jazz

the Prince is positive

        "headline news"

outside
the sun has come to
        kill time

the birds are tweeting to one
another from
        safe distances

my phone
has become my best friend
which makes me

        sick

day 11

the main drag through town
          ghostlike //
                    barren

a police van trails me to
the roundabout
          a temporary digital sign flashing
                    stay home! save lives!

the engine of the world
has stopped
          i can’t help but think
transfixed
by empty windows
          shuttered storefronts
signs of apology attached to letterboxes
                    & lampposts

i wear a mask in Morrisons
wait for people to
leave the aisles before
scuttering through
          holding my breath

we observe each other like
                    an unfamiliar race

wariness & distrust
          bubbling

uneasy
it's a lottery

malevolent droplets

the PM
cooped up with symptoms
says things will get worse
before
anything gets better

day 12

my inbox beeps

          a message from America

John Prine is critical
covid again
& i recall that genius first record
a vision rising
          above Blake's weary
                    eyes

          &
things have got really
                    weird today

that rush of blood realisation
incessant caged delirium
silent // howling // calm

                              foreboding

put the kettle on
                    Mum asks
          with a sigh

day 13

they've built the biggest hospital
on the planet
        & they're calling it
intervention

the guy was grinning as
he showed us round
        on the 6pm national news
somehow immune from
        terror

& they've sent planes to collect
stranded Brits abroad
        with a £75 million tab

bringing them back to
        dystopia

i take a drive
        masked & gloved
no-one around
just an addict scurrying through
        Queen's gardens
looking for scraps

not a face to be seen in windows
        or a voice
            in the breeze

day 16

i am redundant of
my days on the coastline

my boxer dog stares
        at me with those eyes

she hasn’t seen a field
    for weeks

i sit beneath
the same bookcase
in the same room for
every video call
        to the same people
who sit with the same backdrop
    talking the same shit

our days are stretched upon the rack

i always wanted my own
studio // a place to hide away
where sound & vision
        could climb the walls

        a talisman
far from the fearless fat rats
beggars & palmists & pimps & pushers

away from the 9 to 5

& the dread & the mindless
capitalist feast

none of it matters right now

this is survival

wartime spirit in the streets
clapping // car-horns // cheering // bagpipes
from every doorway
at 8pm
tears & heavy breaths
though no-one can quite describe
what it is they feel

there is new-born apprehension

teenagers //
celebrities

invisible demise is indiscriminate

my friend messages me
women troubles
he's been on tinder again stalking
miss tonight

there's more important shit to think about
i reply
& besides, get off the apps

he asks why…

because a woman's voice
is more than half
of love

the virus holds one million captive
worldwide

they say tests are arriving
though vital drugs are waning

in the Philippines
Duterte says he will
bury those who violate
quarantine law
& holds his youth in cages

there is no end to the panic yet

some suggest we've not even reached
the start

i consider
the killer
dressed as droplets
surfing spaces between us –

fate
needs an accomplice

day 18

guttural wheeze
diverting honey coloured eyes

head thrust back
// holding on

a video
from the bed of ICU

from the brink

the very edge of providence
a voice scarred by gasps

don't go out…

this is worse than you can ever imagine

the journey

…has changed

today i wander
          to the bathroom
lather & rinse at my own pace
bathe the sleep from
          shadow stained eyes
brush fuzzy teeth without urgency
there is no clock holding
          me ransom

today i amble downstairs
into silence
where otherwise skitter-scatter rushing
          feet would clatter
take rest upon
a bar stool at the kitchen counter
watch the kettle steam
     & chortle
smooth butter onto crumpets as if
          stroking canvases

today i mosey into
a still garden
          within my castle walls
set up with coffee // book // laptop
under gazebo shade
          watch the queen bee peruse
warming spring delights

let the minutes drain
steadily
into afternoon

today i retire to
the living room
nuzzle with the dog
in front of Netflix
feet elevated
a dash of rioja // home-cooked korma
watch barren streets slide &
surrender to dusk

the city
is already a memory

a fond one at that –

the buzz of train platforms
rustle of bags
voices // car exhausts
common goodbyes
somewhere to be

midnight arrives like
any other double-fingered
milestone

i check the menu
pick out another unfamiliar horror

PLAY

day 31

maybe we will find
another world
          for the blackbird

maybe the Aquarian age is
the last // the best
          or just the beginning

maybe those asking what their country
        can do for them
will answer for themselves
since only dead men
          are free
               from lies

maybe John Lee Hooker
          is playing with thunder
far above cobalt sky
     april lights

maybe the murder in
               these molecules
will raise nations from their knees

maybe my tell-tale heart
will show the scars of separation
as we navigate black
                    dreamlands

maybe those with fingers
on triggers
will stop calculating lives with
just numbers

maybe these gorgeous sickly-silly
love songs
drifting over fences
will make us feel as though
today
is just another day

day 32

their deceit has washed up
on the shore

cracks // like spider mesh forming
on the casing of
fraudulent fat bubbles

the barefoot power of
the masses
are standing on shoulders
rising from the depths of despotic
cultural anaesthetic

with every casualty
thousands rise

no more silent death &
deception

Gaga has them singing from their mansions
tonight

muting the colour of trepidation
for just
a little something more
than complete
annihilation

day 41

         & most folk
stayed at home // followed the rules

prayed for an end in sight
took up new hobbies
binged on Netflix
        had a lie-in (or two)
spent valued time
            with the kids

took a deep breath
         // time to stare at the walls

made phone-calls
         we'd been meaning
to make for months

         started to write

walked for miles
made waves with DIY
lived out life
      on Instagram
chatting // imagining
                  // procrastinating

read that book they
                  always needed to

sang some songs

danced to the heartbeat of a stranded
nation

talked with meaning &
tended the garden with
undiscovered pride

took a drink // stayed up late

rested
healed
pressed reset

started to think about
things
a little differently

like they always hoped they might
given the chance

day 48

down to the beach
for sunset

daily exercise

an eager boxer dog
shivering // excited
yanking leather

i glance over
at the corner house
on the bend

read a kids painting in the window

after storms
come rainbows
it says

& everything inside me
somersaults

twice

day 67

the month of may
has brought leaves
aflame

the same bedroom window
a canvas now

colours & sun
& speckles of hope
glittering in the branches
of our apple tree

there is talk of life reopening

i for one
am listening

day 69

it's
all insane

        that's my
moon-rimmed core-rotten
                appraisal

UFOs
in broad daylight
above filthy
            marina mutating
                beneath

this
bloodied town
below
a weak stone sun
            thumping cancer rays
towards
balding skulls in
              garden cages

the
daily briefing
            soured by nepotism
tells us all the things
we need
    to un-know

the butterscotch
    ice-cream has
ran out…again

what farce!
someone bellows
from
a nearby window

        the story
of our twisted-wheel dystopian
    dreamscape

day 70

ten weeks
hiding from killer
droplets
cute as microscopic rain

deadly as bullets

ten weeks curling pages away
from the sun:

Hemingway, Celiné, Duffy, Bukowski, Steinbeck
Dostoevsky, McCullers, Collins, Angelou
Tolstoy, Camus, Bellow, Fante, Orwell
Plath, Melville, Kafka, Harwood

ten weeks
spinning dusty discs:

Nick Drake, Rival Sons, Nina Simone, David Crosby
Miles Davis, Bonnie Raitt, Soft Machine, Steely Dan
Carole King, Frank Sinatra, Zero 7, Beach Boys
Donna Summer, Rage Against The Machine
Christine & The Queens, Paul Kappa, Boz Scaggs
Leon Russell, Norah Jones, Bert Jansch, Sade
Turin Brakes, Micayl, Lambchop, Liverpool Express
Rolling Stones, Lyle Lovett, Barbara Streisand
Supergrass, The Inkspots, Tangerine Dream
Scott Matthews, Rumer, Tony Bennett

London Grammar, Tom Russell, Fun Lovin' Criminals
Traffic, Judy Collins, Four Tops, Black Sabbath
PJ Harvey, Television, Tash Sultana, Cold Chisel

ten weeks
sucking up subversive propagandist shit
from pretenders-in-chief

ten weeks
reliving wrestling reruns:

- Hogan slamming Andre
- Warrior winning the title // Wrestlemania VI
- Savage & Miss Elizabeth reunited
- Montreal screw-job
- Owen Heart's in-ring death
- Mankind flying off the Hell-in-a-Cell
- Undertaker's streak

ten weeks
learning to reassess

learning to…

ten weeks
walking sunset miles
& miles & miles & miles
with a boxer dog
that's never known it so good –

full clan in tact to
love & protect

ten weeks inside the skin
of these four walls
waiting for the bell
          to ring

one eye on the daily news

     the other on
a cracked moon going
               round & round

          ten weeks
of late nights lost in Netflix:

American Horror Story, Tiger King, Troll Hunter, IT
Blue Velvet, Gerald's Game, Stranger Things
Don't Fuck With Cats, Rolling Thunder Revue
The Never Ending Story, As Above So Below
Left Behind, The Fear of 13, Ghost, Rick & Morty
What Happened Miss Simone?
Humanoids of the Deep, Prank Encounters
The Invitation, Zoo, Jeepers Creepers

ten weeks
     learning
          to
          be

day 73

i
finally get to sleep
after the sky
has stuck
its silver needles through
the blinds

4:48am

i wake with a start

6:32am

dreaming about
our humanity climbing
out the ass
of this dystopian
shit-show

the sun raging
like
a banished angel
i
settle back
into half-sleep

wake again
8:14am

neck cramped
same old cardboard ceiling
same xylophonic
everything

the face
of another day
held under water
panicked gasps
for breath

the gap between
despair & hope
slimmer than those gold-stained shards
of blazing light
screaming at my window

i lean over

click PLAY

lie back
to the sound
of Prince
welcoming
the day

day 81

rain lashed my face
reddened my chapped nose
bruised my enthusiasm
though
i was determined to get out
walk the coastline
// *feel* again

the golden ‘m’ was relit
a saturated synthetic UFO on a quiet skyline
enshrined by derelict factory units
queues round the block for
the drive-thru
young couples
stacked in car-park shelves
feet on the dashboard
lost in the delayed tastes of
our culture

#BLM
scrawled across
the sea wall

a message from the centuries
finally reaching
home

day 82

a petite
hairline crack
has finally split the foundations

the world is dancing heavy
to protest songs
on worn
& bloody feet

the rabbit // eyes bulging
as smoking wheels
roll through
its tiny life

Boris Johnson's
hair ablaze
with dishonour & defeat

Trump has
savaged the dream
& "mob" revolutionaries
scarred // titillated by
the injustices of a bleak history
have surrounded
a white house
that has
never looked so
dark

they keep telling us:

        this is the new normal
this is the new normal this is the new normal
this is the new normal
this is the new normal this is the new normal
        this is the new normal
this is the new normal this is the new normal
this is the new normal
this is the new normal
this is the new normal this is the new normal
        this is the new normal this is the new normal
this is the new normal

this is…

day 83

my
friend
called today
to tell me that
he's on prozac for a
while

it's for the best

i look out at the north star
& the ravens sweeping
the horizon like a besom –

wonder what the world
will look like
when deities
awake //

flip the switch

fragments

[1999-2024]

things can change

i don’t
chase the strobe light
          anymore

all i need
is lamplight instead

the soft heave & sigh
of your chest as
you read
to me from dusty
          books

headlights climbing blinds
somewhere
          past midnight
when words
have settled softly
on the sheets

shame

it’s dark inside
which suits me

it hides my imperfections

the guilt upon my skin
the dread in my eyes
as they size me up

the red lights make their
faces look like death

their touch a shock
beyond disgust

i don’t know
what i’m doing here
but i can’t control it

i roam through narrow passageways
lined with filthy secrets

there’s a world above
tumbling through time
that may never know

i find the flesh i’ve been
looking for

they follow me

i spill my vulnerability
        onto asphalt

recall my Grandfather

what would he think?

we're all the same when we're
          fucking

we lay it down in
languages we cannot understand
exchanging nothing
                    but fluid

i leave empty

          & you begin again

somewhere in the countryside

the barge pulled into dock voices of
those on-board joyful

the clink of glasses a toast to returning
friends sweet memories life

standing outside the situation
raising eyes from wet palms

the agony of calm the stillness of
meadows stretched out over deep
contours like rugs of olive-rusty browns &
golds & auburn tan

spring is in the air cold draught blowing
through the stairwell as i return to
locked doors a note hanging limp
inside the letter box

you never called me it says

i rattle keys lock the world out
for another night

malbec wine & single malt playing with
the poem under lucid carrot glow

listening to Tony Bennett

electric fan buzzing

an inflamed porthole
warming me
from the ankle up

& i never will i scribble // sign
slip into an envelope

a lone farmhouse just the outline
through the study window
standing its ground
at dusk

such a pretty picture

hearts pounding
late-afternoon haze feeding
the spaces
between tall
black pines

it began
as
just a passing
thought in the cheap
slender kitchen

friends who had
become strangers

too much booze

the passing
of years
stitched with
the ruffling of a dog's ears

the wild country it's a painting
on your wall

the kind
you want to step
inside

colossal trunk
        blocking pathways to
the other side   saplings fending
        off silver rays with
                khaki shields

        the
entry to a million
                myths or truths

he
retrieves
the ball
& i throw it
further
    than before

                voices in the air
        warning me not to overstay

begging me
        to never leave

dissident

i find myself
in Manchester again

this time
a business meeting
last time
a poetry reading
                    a gig
       an exhibition

coffee
with old friends

off to watch the cricket
pub crawl with the old university crowd
former lecturer's book launch
friend's birthday
          freebie at the football match
      stag do
head-wetting bevvies
shopping trip for
              that new record

          i've thought
about these yarns i've spun
paralysed by a life
                    you'll never
          understand

huddled
in front of pornography
in common rooms
full
of walking
          secrets

stalking basements lined
        with cats eyes
            of
alarm bell reds
          to help intimate strangers
                  who are lost
                          to
                    find
                      their
                          way

i saw it all coming
more vividly
        than it's happening

            i knew
that you would end up
idolising me
      in ways that would destroy
                    us both

i'm still finding reason to
          blame you for the things
you don't even know

the air is thick in
            these places
& no amount
of showering can clean
      shame
from your pores
or
chlorine from
      your pruned creases

the primal recurring lust
              that sweating walls
       lined with skin
            arouses

walking out onto unlit streets
          5:38am
scanning empty car parks
for trouble

      body redundant
of sleep

          coffee is a blessing
& the first train
    out of the station
rattles   mostly empty
       through freezing
              fog

back towards the sham
                   that is our reality

this is what they've done

i've cried a lot today i can feel change

life is full of change

change doesn't come easy

i've been forced into change

they've made me feel like i've achieved nothing

they see success in terms of money
& i have no money left

today it's hit me everything is changing

the air the sky it all seems different

i have to take breaks from packing my case

i can't listen to these records anymore

tonight is the last time i'll sleep in my bed

the dog keeps looking at me

everything is changing

music used to live here

gliding with the owls at dusk
in search of freshwater

this is how you break a child:

a) let them fly too early

b) never show them that they have wings

c) take the Mother away

(one is enough   two, almost certainty
three, well . . .)

music used to live here

lying upon mountains   silence
recollections   violence

this place i'm in
this space we breathe

graft my layers away
find me   forgotten
the crust
brittle // fucked

i am no artist

put that record on

'Put that record on,' she said, falling through my bedroom door.

'Which one?'

'That one I really love.'

Balanced over the edge of the bed, I reached for the CD and flipped it into the player. She crashed onto the stacked cushions, spilling a little gin.

'You should stop drinking so much.'

'Bollocks,' she scowled.

The record came on. A cotton shawl hung over bony shoulders. She wore a bright blue bob, black lipstick, orange eye-shadow and a tiny pair of denim shorts. Her tights were laddered from the calf up. She smelt like coconut and mandarin and rum.

'Love the socks,' she chuckled.

I looked down. I hadn't even realised. Christmas socks in February.

Take me out tonight...take me anywhere, I don't care, I don't care, I don't care...

She splashed her drink down perilously close to my brand new copy of *Ulysses* and pulled me up by the wrists.

'Dance with me.'

'It's not really dance music,' I said.

'Dance with me!'

She leant over and switched off the lamp. Silhouettes in a terraced bay window swaying to The Smiths in the moonlight. She gasped with pleasure, eyes closed, leaning back against the weight of my shoulder. Her acrid exhalations invaded my nostrils, and I noticed how frail she seemed for a twenty-year old.

The record finished and she fell back on the bed. I heard the front door slam.

'I'm home!' Kevin, my flatmate, shouted, poking his head round my bedroom door. He looked down at Cassie and shook his head.

'How was it?' I asked. He'd just done his final exam of the semester.

'Rough,' he sighed.

The headlights of an HGV swept across the street and the sound of someone laughing fell through the window, slightly ajar, despite the cold.

'Put that record on again,' Cassie slurred. Kevin rolled his finger round his temple. *Nuts.*

I put it on anyway.

...and in a darkened underpass I thought, oh God, my chance has come at last...

She rolled over, curled foetal, onto my pillows. By the end of the song she was asleep, her chest rising calmly, her shorts wedged high on her thighs revealing every groove and bow.

I'd be sleeping on the sofa again.

I walked into the kitchen where Kevin was pouring two tequilas. He looked at me and laughed.

'You never learn,' he said, handing me the drink.

that thing they can't abide

every time we
touch
i get that sinking feeling
        in my gut

the sort you get
when police sirens illuminate the streets behind you
        on an empty country road
                late evening

the sort you get at airport security
when buzzers & lights
& alarms flash

... just step over here please, sir...

the sort you get when the landline rings
        in the middle of the night

& what breaks my heart
is that you look at me
        like everything i've just
                explained
        is happening
to you too

northern towns in winter

the fragments somehow disparate
erotic the meaning of these relationships
you & me streets that we
walk down // they die
upon

the moon stays longer until midday
kids crowd the pier despite two degree
gales

i am thinking of you // i am with you
photographs the gentleness of strangers
indigent devotion

peppermint ice-cream cone gripped by gloves
i stare up at the tower burgundy antique
images & allures
they crowd the penny arcade

small daily things nothing to anyone

one day i'll tell you the truth

journey to Snowdonia

there isn't much traffic on the road at
4:30am roads that usually carry
the mass of rush-hour

we cruise
past overnight lorries on
the carriageway
soothing early morning
radio moulding us
into heated seats

petite droplets of fine-rain painting windscreens
as you smile

is that really Ben E. King?
we laugh
vibing with the bass upon
ghost motorways light dribbling through
the greys & shadows of cities in
the valleys

we pull in
amongst station wagons parked up on
gravel curtains drawn across
cabins // across solitary lives

the crisp crackle
of frying bacon local voices

i hold a steaming black coffee in
two chilled hands watching
onions bubble

you take me
by the shoulder

i can drive from here

clouds forming
over mountains
the morning air   pain of intimacy
precision of your touch

& i am
no longer sure
about much

cross country

there were memories falling from
your pockets
in
the back carriage
of the 11:57am going west

i met your side profile
dressed in dulled countryside insignias
            & jagged rays
        at least a dozen times

those eyes a banquet of
        trouble

i watched you get off
    at Crewe
knowing that was it
            for us

knowing that a hospital for broken hearts
would declare us both
                    terminal
    without ever really
                knowing why

it's only belief

what else can words do
but love eventually?

sacrifice your edges
plummet into me the city
looking on

let me complete you
let me be your art &
brush your strokes across my world
filling in the cavities

the sea is quiet

the coves chiselled into faces
hide us
the sounds of love

we're here which sounds curt
i know
in this room full of mirrors

only astronauts
& something much greater than
the force of love
overlooking these
imperfections

the last night of our lives

your shoulder blades
danced
as you entered
          the waves
                    naked // drunk

i followed
          illuminated
by the moon
fantasising
that we might stay
afloat
    forever

or
at the very least
drown
together

ruminations

the sculpted lines around your eyes
chiselled dimples cavernous reminders
of something less than
satisfaction

maybe i pulled at your
strings
too hard smothered you with disregard
made you believe in things
i could never follow through

things like this: me // you

i shunned things my Mother
said about
love about *me*

ripped you shut from throat
to chest
with
nothing but …
// everything but … affection

gave *them* everything // nothing
they'd crave
without sincerity

isn't that just like me?

melancholy

i drew
the curtains
& waited for days

when
i opened them
again
i had no idea
what i'd
been waiting for

songwriting

the tunes are spilling
out
of me

because everything else
is sinking
    in

at dusk in the city

you will hear the sirens
& think
they are for
you

snap retinas back & forth
in haste
searching
for the sound

5am traffic spinning through
flashing lights happy to sweep
the day in offices // factories
retail outlets
off their shoulders
like dandruff

the portly guy in
the hot dog trailer
shivering-warm over
steaming stainless steel
will tell you
fucking hell, mate, it's been a
slow one
as he passes you the mustard
thinking all the while
about his wife how she'll flip if he stops for
a bevvie on the way home

today the
streets will scatter
        like bomb-threats
    when freezing hail
        arrives   only the *Big Issue* guy
            hunched in layers
        remains
  thrusting bundles
wrapped in plastic at folk
        who
dance with umbrellas like tiger cubs
        in competition

      mental   you will gasp
falling through the door   heavy bags
                    etching lines
            upon your wrist

reflected in puddles

locals gather   centre of the village

an old man flying kites
high above the square
which is
small // somehow Oriental

she stops to sit
beneath the fingers of a husky oak

a postcard to a lover

. . . it rains heavily here but
the town is like a painting . . .

long september nearly over   coastal pathways
down to hotels snaking past pier
heads & fishing boats
translation of Tristan Tzara under
her arm

. . . i miss you & i love you
but i may never understand you . . .

at night her window
open wide

the scent of falling
dew outside

all i'm thinking about

    the trees in
huckleberry grove were
        touching their toes in the gusts
so we drove down to
the coast
where boats bobbed
drunk in the storm
& waves curled like hands
scraping back
        the sand

who'd have known
that later
when clouds exploded
science-fiction electric white
we would be sat
on benches // walking through pathways
        where birds howl
resting in the hairy dunes at Crosby beach
everything calm
            for now

the only threat   this happiness
the splendour in the scattered constellations
        as planets dance towards
                tomorrow

unreachable

the continents
            have become
small strides
i have trembled upon

we've
ogled peaks &
breathed the darkness
            of lairs

witnessed peaceful
      dawns
skimming damp off
powder clouds

with wings bound
for somewhere
i've pierced the
            hum & haze
of a thousand
       cities

with hardened feet &
softened eyes
      i have trodden
the pathways
of legends
            & lunatics

gripped the same bars
as spirits
scratching at the years
        to get back

ridden time-zones
        like roller coasters

held a hundred faceless loves
            wondering
                    is this it?

watched youth roll away
& gently return
(from time to time)
like tides
bound to disperse by
        morning

written words like these
just to hang on &
    maybe believe it all

i've done all that
        probably more

though every step i take
towards you & yours
        always
takes me further & further

        & further away

building nests in the country

watching rain crack glass

i love the conservatory overlooking forestlands
of birch & hazel & hornbeam

we are here // together // a kind of alone
you warm the milk the coffee is steaming
dull lamps radiating
turntable spinning

it's nice…what is it?

you hold vinyl into sharp light
it's French you smile
1958

the clock says afternoon but it feels
like now

you point acutely

a hawfinch hiding in birdhouses
at the end of
the garden

at the end of its life

seasons

another evening stalking
24-hour supermarkets for
a reason to live

unemployed & undersexed the rain
over the hills vicious
// beautiful

i might fall in love on a train
or die waiting

i might find you hidden in choruses or
the masquerade where i can
pull off this guise
head to the moors // smoke the sky
taste auburn greens & never
have to wonder why

the streets are narrow these days
allegories landscapes
smoky bars & jukebox queens
killers in cafes
at dawn

i'll keep coming for you
keep wandering
these desolate moors
these poems
& these metaphors

college nights & days

standing on the edge of
barricades   rain falling on his shoes

3am   petrol station lights

laughter in the alleys
the mathematician fucking the rich kid
up against Mary Blaine
beloved wife & Mother
b.1863 – d.1937

doormen gathering   sirens

she was half in love on the avenue
leaning   boy with man's hands // chrome wheels
relax, don't do it   the late-bar
dying with the hour
late november fog curling round car parks &
warehouses like clenched fists

streets waking up   garlic mayo under
fingernails
hypnotic fruit machine jangle
medium or large?
no taxis // no jackets // blowing air into
blueing hands

what you lookin at lad?
temples   breath   guts   anus

all in bits

fall asleep cock in hand
headphones in

her face with him
alarm alarm alarm MOTHER
alarm MOTHER

you were late

undulating country roads
hedges scraping // whipping windows
bloody traffic lights
every single one

no texts the emptiness of it all stripping
his insides

sausage barm no sauce
everyone fucked

she appears from somewhere deep inside of him

this town is cancerous she whispers
rolled-up cigarette // double-shot espresso
purple-yellowed eye somewhere between
exhaustion & submission

did he do it? i don't ask
(he's somewhere in the canteen)

a thick black knitted jersey hanging
fleshless shoulders
flakes of skin like trapped flies
scatty hair // barb-wire knots
// gnawed nails

beautiful

pool balls click the notice says no tobacco in
the common room she rolls another
Stooges on the jukebox
The Cure on the jukebox
Lou Reed on the jukebox

did you see the graffiti? she forces smiles
legs crossed // twitchy
by him? i do say it

i do say it

drilling in the walls two middle-aged
overalls grin
they've picked the ones they'd love to screw

yeah she mouths

by him

Hemingway

words somehow husky
heavy light scent of monte cristos
clinging to aged oak

they taste something like bittersweet
feel to touch like melancholy

grip me
like a man

it's never too late

don't fall
for the same denigrations
time & time
        & time again

don't sell your flesh
            at rich men's markets

don't let them in
            before you open the
                        door

don't give your adoration to
            those incapable
                        of affection

                        &

            don't
feast your eyes on the prize
if there's nothing
            behind the prize
                    but lies

even
on a sunday

recovery

i want to
pick wounds
from your
flesh
like splinters
so
that
i
can put
you back into
the world

bold

immaculate

music

bring all your bombs
bring your rocket launchers

bring all the ammunition
                the DMZ can muster

bring the submarines
the ultramarines
bring the secret service
MI5 // FBI // KGB
bring the whole damn lot

bring all the
hurricanes & earthquakes
Mother nature can
          unleash

bring the great floods
the typhoons
the twisters
          & monsoons

the grizzly bears
          & great white sharks
tigers // lions // hippos // rhinos
vipers // black widows
                    anacondas
crocodiles & jelly-fish

bring malaria with
                    the mosquito
bring rabies with
      the wolf
bring the buffalo
the bow & arrow
            & the hand-grenades

bring the fiercest of the extinct
the tyrannosaurus
the raptors
            & sea monsters of
                  the ages

bring the Jesuits // the Muslims
                        the Hindus & the Sikhs &
            the Buddhist monks

            hell
just bring everybody

bring the serial killers
the story tellers
the dictators // totalitarians
the Maasai tribes
            & the barbarians

bring the saviours
            the rock & rollers
bring the vagabonds & tagalongs
bring all the Greek Gods
                        & the devil himself

bring them all, why don’t you?

the awesome

the unimaginable

bring the
power
of those
opening notes
feeding the
silence
like a sweet sweet

apocalypse

decay

There was no doubt he'd changed.

People were repelled by him. His instinct had become rage.

He knew it, but pretended he didn't.

Everyone he met felt the heat. Something could go off at any minute. People don't need that. People seek shade when fires burn too hot.

The expressions on his face were ugly. He couldn't seem to lift the corners of his mouth, or level the concave right eyebrow that painted permanently rugged sneers.

There is energy within a soul that spills out on the floor, puddles in corners, climbs walls, glows like spider webs in the lofty crooks and bends of a ceiling. It glistens or it pulses or it damn well deters. He hated himself. Hated pretty much everyone else.

Age had done this to him.

He was nearly forty now. You can lean forward however far you want, but you can't reach back. It's gone. He despised that perpetual, damning reality.

Sideburns turning grey, full face and chin, rolls on the hips, cracked hands, birthdays without meaning. It was a conspiracy he couldn't accept. There were fewer office romances, fewer glances on the tube. It had to be people that caused it. People and days and the streets and the daily news.

What left was there to love?

A man at nearly forty is neither young or old, or anything at all, unless it's engineered. A man without youth, or enough experience, is a derelict building. A tin box without a lid. A man who can't dance for shit can't hit the floor.

When chances at love came he mistook it for cunning.

His bedroom had become a cemetery.

We only ever sleep alone.

itinerant

at once they branded me “the medium”
i eloped not wanting to
assume such labels

not wanting them wielding their
Bibles // Qurans // Vedas // Tripitakas

all that was left
burrowing
in roadside hovels

learning to live without ever looking up

waiting for ill portent
to signal time

the hunt for
something
must resume

market day

they pick herbs from local gardens
fresh fish from the pier
the best rump steak from old Joe's farm
veggies with a sheen from
        dawn markets on the promenade

picking the best is artistry   he smiled
cupping gleaming caulies & broccoli stems like trophies
placing them in his basket as though
        newborn pups

it made me glad to be back in England
watching 5am smiles pulling
        away in ageing cosy vans

waving at the competition

tender white rollers lapping the edge
of the cove like tongues
                eager to be fed

the skylark & the boy

the skylark is speaking you said
hushing me with the pad
of your forefinger

i loved you at that moment
on the banks of
the ribble estuary
the breeze
a sultry off-white

*

killing me came as a surprise
in the november (i think)
she's done this to you Mother said
roaring through emphysema in the
post office queue

it was pointless arguing

*

it's a shame we have to die
derek said

get away from that boy
his Mum said
fingering the lingerie in m&s

our egypt project failed
at school
though derek put most of the work in

Mum didn't have enough
fish fingers to have him round anyway

but he could have
had some of mine

*

what did it say i whisper

years later

*

i am the post office clerk

& we all thought she was
going to hit him
which has happened before
but never before lunch

*

tonight I'm going to drink myself insane
maybe do a line or two

*

don't hit him i kept thinking
he didn't look a full mix
that one

tall though
got some shoulders on him

those trousers looked
a little short
grubby too

*

holy shit, is it friday *again*?

*

best not push him

he's strong

thighs like bravery
chest like
dynamite

*

strike a pose
throw some shapes
breathe in the flashes
dodge
the scrapes

*

first class, madam?

whatever

*

i am 'you' to him // 'she' to her

walking
is my favourite thing
especially in the afternoon

i like to imagine yesterday
i like to imagine Paris
i like to imagine sundays
sometime in may
i like to think of passion as
time // silence // music
i like to dream of wings
& many things
almost anything

he speaks

it turns silence
to chaos

he
has to go

*

Mother

they never think about the hearts
of men
these girls about town

they are just plasticine

*

i'm not derek's biological Mum

this town is getting worse

you should have heard
this woman curse!

grotesque // no makeup
a tatty head of grease & grey
& a walking stick a *walking* stick!
must be my age huh!
should be ashamed

& as for that boy that smelly excuse
for a teenage boy
to me he looked a touch deranged

oh, i told him! don't you worry
i said *derek! get away from that boy!*
before you catch something!

before he steals something!

by the way
amanda was in the coffee house
botox bitch
they've bought a beige 4x4…

*

most call me des

i'm sad for him
that's all

i'd like to be his friend
if only she'd allow it

he likes to talk & walk
& if you get him to walk
he'll talk

it's nice to talk
to someone
isn't it?

*

skylark

as if telling him
would ever make a difference
anyway

i think i'll call it morning

The wheels flirted with the runway a few times before that jagged bump that fills everyone with apprehension. I always take the wing since tall, strong, young guys travelling alone can talk their way into an exit seat at check-in. Especially if they're willing to smile.

'That was rough,' the odd lady sitting next to me said to nobody, so everyone could hear.

I watched the wing shake with tension, then that moment of relief when the brakes grip.

The cabin crew had expressionless faces, and I wondered what it must be like to work above the clouds.

'Well, I guess we're here,' the odd lady commentated.

'I guess we are,' I said, which she ignored.

The weather in Manchester is rarely welcoming. Specks of rain gathered on my cabin window.

The time in Manchester is 8:42am, and the weather, as you can see, cold and wet, with a temperature outside of six degrees Celsius. That's 42 degrees Fahrenheit.

There was a rush when the seatbelt sign flicked off, but I didn't move. It didn't matter how fast you got your bag down. Experience taught me that. What mattered was how fast you could walk the vacuous, antiseptic smelling corridors to immigration.

'Hello, sir,' the officer smiled. They rarely smile.

'Hello.'

'Please stand back a pace for the photo.'

I stood back, arms folded behind me, like a school year photograph. The officer next door asked mine a question. A brief moment of distraction left me lingering. Something to do with the printing machine. My officer exited his booth and walked around to help, and I was left wondering if they were looking at pictures of me on the screen – all the things I'd never done.

'Sorry for the delay,' he smiled, returning to his seat. The stamp came down and the robotic glass gateway opened.

Relief.

My case came quickly. I spotted it on the conveyor belt from a distance - my old skull and crossbones bandana tied around the handle.

'It's a myth, you know.'

'Sorry?' I said, turning to face the old man leaning on his trolley.

'Manchester. It's a myth. It's not the wettest city here like everyone thinks.'

I smiled, nodded, then walked over to claim my case. There was a fragile label stuck on it because of my ukulele. My pulling weapon, as I'd tell my mates on our email syndicate. No need for chat up lines when you can play the little conjurer and sing along. *Wow, that's so cool.* Two hours later, hearts pounding in cosy beach alcoves just far enough away from the music, with only the moon bearing witness.

'You look so well!' my Mum lied, throwing her arms around me.

'I'm tired,' I smiled. 'Where's Dad?'

'In the car.'

The smell of bakery, and coffee, and sharp, pungent shit from the nearby toilets decorated the air. Mum grimaced but would never comment on anything so crude.

'Hungry?' she asked.

'I was,' I laughed, and that was enough.

We walked under the sheltered walkway, the restful sound of gentle rain pattering the plastic. Mum kept turning to check I was really there.

'Typical Manchester,' she laughed.

'Not necessarily so,' I began, then stopped.

'Sorry?'

'Nothing, Mum.'

***

Rain. Glorious rain.

I like to make love in the rain, Miranda said, or so I thought, caressing my nipple with her forefinger under my baggy Jim Morrison vest. Her blazing red, voluminous curls danced as she flicked her head side-to-side, riding through thick, gluey inebriation.

'I'm Dutch,' she said, snaking her finger deeper into my weakness.

'Ok,' I managed, smitten by stars.

The last stop, Ko Pha Ngan, was mental. Thailand was mental. The whole of Asia had been mental. I was glad I'd finally been and ticked the Full Moon Party off my bucket list, but even gladder it was over. My skin was still dry, and my eyes swollen from sleep deprivation. I was ten pounds lighter, and I could see it in my cheeks.

'There's no rain here,' I mouthed at Miranda, and we fucked like two nations at war.

***

'It's so expensive to park here!' Mum said, searching the bowels of her handbag for change.

'I can't help you,' I grinned, waving a Thai note and noticing the eight pound fee on the ticket machine.

'We were a little early,' she grimaced.

Dad was conservative as ever. We exchanged an awkward half-hug. He looked older to me, especially round the eyes. Slower too, with veins protruding on his temples. Four years is a long time.

'Here's a chewing gum,' he said, his worn hand shaking a little.

England looked so small to me now. The buildings, the scope, the roads. Even the motorways seemed narrow and claustrophobic, especially the M6. I never liked that motorway. We jutted off onto the B-roads, and I overlooked the fields running into the horizon like a sloppy oil painting.

'My eyes feel strange,' I said.

'How was the flight?' Mum asked.

'Same as ever.'

Nobody really knew what that meant.

Mum wouldn't fly. Dad had to drive down to Southampton so they could hop on cruises if they wanted to go abroad. She point-blank refused. *I'm not riding a sardine can with wings*, she liked to say, chuckling. *Cars and bears and alcohol kill more*, I'd say.

'I don't know how you do it,' she muttered, shaking her head.

We reached home in under an hour, and my Sister was sitting waiting with our boxer dog, who recognised me instantly. Her little bum wiggled uncontrollably, and she licked me over and over. Her ears were flat with joy at my returning, recognisable scent. Her nose and eyes were grey too. *That son-of-a-bitch-colour gets everyone*, I thought.

'So skinny!' my Sister laughed, pressing a gift at me after pulling me in tight. I unwrapped it, the dog pulling at the rogue ends like a madwoman. Tom Petty – *An American Treasure*. Nice.

'He died while you were away.'

'Sad,' I agreed, leafing through the booklet.

Nan was in the kitchen, banging and crashing the pots, not realising we'd arrived.

'She's cooking hot-pot,' Mum smiled. 'Deaf as a doornail.'

'Don't frighten her,' Dad said, stripping off his layers.

Mum shouted her and she came in, beaming. She was heavier, but looked better for it. Her cheeks were flushed and she looked healthy. Eighty-six years old.

'Oh, my boy!'

Nan cried a little, which started Mum off.

The hot-pot was a treat, and Nan never stopped smiling. My Sister stayed to eat too, and I told them stories about Cambodian temples; the Indian kids I played cricket with in the streets; the Sri Lankan monsoon I got caught in; the cherry blossom in Japan (Nan sighed longingly); and, the orangutans swinging in the trees of Borneo.

'You've had quite the trip,' Dad said.

'You wouldn't believe half of it,' I grinned.

I told the story of the Indonesian jungle boy who reminded me of Mowgli – our guide through the wilderness – and how he sobbed when I left him with my rucksack full of English books. *Wuthering Heights, Don Quixote, Lolita, Journey To The End Of Night*. He'd never seen books like it, and stroked them with his rugged palms.

'Thank you, friend,' he'd said with red, gloopy eyes, and I cried too.

'They've taken the postbox from the top of our road,' Nan grumbled. 'This country's getting bloody worse!'

Everyone laughed, and somewhere through the window I saw old Bill next door walking up his path with the weekend race review tucked under his arm, just like he always did.

supernatural

i want to write a little poem
with a melody
so we
can rock this child
to sleep

but the spirits hang
like lanterns

pressing on us
          cheek-to-cheek

so did i

i left my heart
in your city
in a paper bag

so be sure
to keep it warm until
          i return

don't leave it near the windowsill
because my time is on
loan & a cold heart won't fit
     within these bones

massage it to the beat of your
          dancing feet

lightly press it
caress it

stoke the embers
lay it down & let it sleep

yours is mine
all in good time

     & mine is yours
to keep

for the purpose of experiment

gather prized possessions
skulk towards windows

toss them onto streets heavy with crushed voices
run wild-eyed down hollow stairs
                    can of petrol in hand

dance around the heap

douse it   *douse it*   *douse it*

strike a match & freeze the scene

        lie amongst cinders
                eyes like spinning plates

wait for howls of black alarms

everything
        in its right place

head in the clouds

i graduated
as the new millennium was
          in its infancy

bounced around
chip on shoulder
expecting admiration

          sat cross-legged
waiting for that rap on the door
golden ticket to a dream job
          // life of luxury

but time ticked on
& before i knew it there were more
          self-important // indoctrinated graduates
                    bounding about town

          more delusion
forever expecting
ceaselessly presuming
& making no concrete plans for their futures
                              just like me

years down the line
& countless brain-abating
                    meaningless jobs later
i sit & wonder where
it all went wrong

why there wasn't anyone to
put their arm around me
& tell me to get off that cloud i was
living on

i needed to know
that there wasn't anything special
about me at all

that the pretence // arrogance // superiority complex
the expectancy & the false dream
was futile

instead
i live embittered
hating the system than funnelled me through
& failed me

& i question
as i see kids like me getting screwed
the same way every year
whether all hope has gone
& whether it was ever really there
in the first place

rags of light: new & unreleased writings

[2023-2024]

bildungsroman

you don’t need me as
your enemy

you don’t need any more enemies

you are your own
worst
    enemy

& one
as
volatile
as that
          is
          all
          you’ll ever need

raw

teach me how beneath this tree
you gasped

i’d never felt
so alive

Blackpool

'Let's go to Blackpool,' Max said.

It was 9:15am, and we were sitting in Maggie's café on Southport Promenade.

'There's meant to be storms later.'

'Storms in Blackpool? Sounds boss if you ask me.'

We could see the famous cast iron Tower and 'Big One' roller coaster across hellish quick-sands that had taken so many lives. My eye traced the jutting edges of the Ribble Estuary, all the way round past Preston, imagining the drive.

'There used to be a hovercraft over to Blackpool,' I said, creating whirlpools in my tea with a plastic spoon.

'We were only kids,' he nodded.

It had always fascinated me - the Tower that is, standing bold on the skyline in the shadow of looming Lake District peaks. It had been years since I'd been to Blackpool. Mum and Dad would take me and my Sister when we were little to see the illuminations, and maybe have a chippy tea. It was so exciting driving there on a school night, wrapped up in duffle coats, knowing we were heading for the lights and the noise and the neon-lit arcades and that exciting carnival atmosphere.

The A59 through Penwortham was surprisingly quiet for a late Saturday morning.

'The footie must be away this week,' Max said.

I checked my phone. Blackpool were away at Rotherham.

'Yeah, they are. Though you'd think the shoppers would be out.'

'Must have heard about the storms,' he said.

I gazed out the window at moody northern seaside skies as we passed through the row of shops on Penwortham high street. Clouds were assembling in the east like a rebel gang. They looked bleak, angry, sinister. An old lady was struggling out of the bakery with her shopping cart, and a young guy doing road works in an ill-fitting hard hat and high-viz took her by the elbow and walked her to the bus stop.

'What a gent,' I smiled.

We curved up the bridge, entering Preston from the south, careful not to get stung by the speed camera cruelly positioned on the sweep. It was too late to see it if you were unfamiliar with the area. A real cheeky one. *Bastards.*

Max shunted us into left hand traffic to avoid heading towards Fishergate, and some bruiser behind slammed his horn, shaking his fist.

I flipped him the finger. '*Cunt.*'

This guy stalked us, bumper to bumper, until flashing past at the start of the dual carriageway. He was mouthing things through his window. We saw the speed camera flash up ahead and laughed.

'Justice is served,' Max hooted, and I jabbed him in the shoulder playfully.

I turned up the radio when Christine and the Queens came on singing *Girlfriend.* Max started dropping his shoulder in time with the beat and tapping his fingers on the wheel. Outside, that bizarre thing happened where the sky goes really dark but the sun seems to shine electric-bright on the ground.

'It's coming,' he sighed.

The deluge hit as we passed exit slips to Lytham St Annes - and I mean it pelted down. A dog walker looked mortified as he sheltered in a cramped bus cabin, hood blowing wildly like a noose pulling him skywards. The poor dog was already drowned. Everyone had their headlights on, though it was barely past midday.

'The sea in Blackpool will be rough,' Max grinned.

'It's deadly in weather like this.'

'Didn't a few people get swept off the North Pier recently?'

'Happens a lot. Terrible when you think about it.'

The roads cleared a little, but traffic was dense as we turned onto Blackpool Promenade. The tram depot was brand new, though it looked like a UFO on the nostalgic promenade. There were very few people around - they'd all legged it indoors when the rains came. We crawled along behind a stack of weary cars, pushing through the blasting downpours like knackered horses on the home straight. It seemed even heavier now without any cover from the Irish Sea.

'Fuck me,' Max gasped, 'that's just wild!'

The Pleasure Beach looked empty. I had to lean across him as he drove to peer up at the 'Big One' through his gale-streaked window. It wasn't running. *Fuck that*, I kept thinking. You'd never get me up there in a month of Sundays.

A tram was crawling past towards the depot – a classic, single-deck Brush Car 621 in khaki green. I couldn't make out the faces on board, but they sat perfectly still, glued to the blizzard outside.

'Let's check-in a B&B,' Max decided.

'Why not,' I agreed. We were a spontaneous pair.

I went on my phone and found a cheap place just behind the Tower. The reviews weren't great, but it was prime location for a messy night out, and we only needed to get our heads down.

'Is there parking?' he asked.

'No, but we'll find somewhere.'

We did. A 24-hour car park for twelve quid. We split the cost and took the hit. Usually you'd think your pants had been pulled down, but it didn't seem too bad for a full night when you broke it down by the hour. The car park literally backed onto Houndshill Shopping Centre too, but we still got soaked running to the entrance. Inside it was packed with shoppers sheltering from the sudden soaking armageddon. We headed to the toilets to dry off under the hand dryers, and I noticed gangs of teens in the food court just hanging around. One of the lads was putting on the swagger in his trackies and the girls were giggling. Another lad had his hands down the front of his pants, and I could see an old lady on the next table tutting to her husband and shaking her head.

The toilet stank of cheap lavender and disinfectant. Something was going on in one of the cubicles, but the cleaner looked too stunned to do anything. Heavy breathing, whispering, and the odd rattle of the thin partition. Max and I looked at one another and laughed.

'What've you got me into here,' he said, squeezing my neck where he knew I was tender. McDonalds was our only option, but Max protested so we got a panini in Starbucks with a strong espresso. We were going to need to feel alive. We had quite a day of drinking ahead.

It was a pleasant Starbucks - very spacious with brand new furniture. It smelt of wood dust, like it had only just been refitted. A group of college types were playing Monopoly on a table in the corner, and a row of young professionals lined the high seats in the window with books and newspapers and mobile phones with ear buds. The barista was cute, with an adorable European lilt. Her smile was genuine, which is rare these days. That sound of blasting steam always warms my bones.

'What's the plan then?'

'Let's get checked in at one, then hit the bars,' Max grinned.

The rain outside stopped, and a calm sun blanketed the streets once again. There were puddles swaying in the gutters, and people emerged from shop doorways wearily. Another gale could turn on this exposed seaside town at any minute. We could hear Irish music coming from a decrepit boozer down a back alley under the Tower. An angular guy with matted hair and filthy fingernails was smoking a roll-up in the doorway. A group of builders, rained off the job, were brushing the water off the chairs outside, pints of lager in their hands.

'Early start for some.'

'Animals,' Max chuckled.

The Tower looked immense from underneath, and memories flooded back. I'd never been up it, but I'd imagined I had in dreams, staring out at the apparitional banks of Ireland and feeling the wind whip my cheeks. We cut down a backstreet to the B&B, and had to ring a bell at the door.

'Hilton here we come,' Max sniggered, and I gave him another dig.

A buzzer went off and the latch released. Inside the narrow lobby the floral browns and purples in the carpet were worn, and the beige wallpaper discoloured from decades of cigarette smoke. A tiny, gaunt guy with badly blackened teeth appeared in the hatch, which was lined with piles of flyers for shows and bars. I picked up a map of the promenade and put it in my pocket.

'Name?' he barked, half coughing. His breath stank stale.

'Cooper.'

'Just you two?'

'Yep.'

'Double room. Is that ok?'

Max and I looked at one another and shrugged.

'Fine.'

The receptionist reached over to a row of hooks where keys were hanging like bodies on a corkboard. They weren't modern keys; more like shed keys nowadays. He thrust them at me, and I got a waft of sour, beefy body odour.

'This is your key. Top floor on the left.' He shuffled them round, exhaling heavily. 'This is the front door key. It's locked after ten at night. Checkout in the morning is eleven.'

He looked so fed up with life I almost felt the terrible urge to hug him, or even kill him.

'No problem.' I took the key and we bolted upstairs.

It was just about the most antwacky place I'd ever seen. Hadn't had a lick of paint since the sixties. There was a strange decaying smell in the corridors, and the staircase creaked like a sluggish brass band.

'Trust you,' Max mocked, pushing me through the door into a small room with a double bed. There was one musty bedside table, a kettle that you wouldn't use if someone paid you, and a waste paper basket draped with a plastic carrier bag from Iceland Supermarket folded inside out. The bracket in the wardrobe was broken. Just as well we had nothing to hang.

Our abode for the night was at the back of the building, and the window overlooked the industrial bins in a scrappy courtyard. Blasts of vapour rose from the pipe on the wall nearby our window. There were two folded towels, both with holes in, and two small soaps wrapped in tacky plastic on the pillows.

'Me first,' Max said, starting to strip down.

I laid my rucksack on the bed and took out my toiletries. The mattress creaked and I could feel the springs, jagged and hardy.

'How much was this?' he frowned, cock already out in the bathroom doorway. His chest looked bigger, like he'd been hammering the weights.

'Thirty-five quid.'

He danced about under the cold shower until it warmed up, buzzing and sputtering noises coming from the meter. He never closed the door when he showered.

'Not bad,' I heard him call, then laugh, through the mist and rap-tap-tap of water hitting the plastic shower curtain.

By the time we made it out it was almost 2pm, and the April sun was warm. We were dressed for an evening out, and Max stank of Creed, which he'd pumped all over himself in the room until I could barely breathe. I had my skinny jeans and converse on, which he said looked cute with my footballer thighs. I'd dug him in the ribs and he'd faked horrendous pain, falling on the bed like he'd been shot.

'Springs have gone!'

He'd covered his face and cackled again, somewhat ironically.

The first pub we went in looked rough outside, but inside it wasn't too bad. A time capsule. We both loved places that were full of characters. A fat guy with a porn star moustache was playing chirpy keyboard to backing tracks, and the strumpet behind the bar was grinding her hips against the stool, half in jest, half believing in herself.

'This is the place,' I said.

We ordered two Guinness and emptied them pretty quickly as several karaoke singers got up, backed by the keyboard porn guy. The barmaid gave me the eye as we ordered two more, though she was probably late forties and wore all the cracks of a woman who'd been through the mill.

'Town bike, that,' some regular whispered in my ear, winking at her as he said it.

She couldn't make out through the music what he'd said, though I don't suppose she cared. She swept back her greasy greying curls and thrust her chest out as she took my money. I gave her a tip, and she mouthed *thanks honey*.

An odd looking guy in a stiff collared leather jacket was called up for karaoke. He'd been sitting on his own with a pint of lager covered by a beer mat. He was checking himself out in a tiny mirror sewn into the inside lapel of his jacket when we walked in. Max had nudged me and nodded in his direction. Our eyes had met as he was spitting on his fingers and sweeping what was left of his fringe back. Awkward.

'Roy's gonna sing *Psycho Killer*!' keyboard porn shouted, and the few locals cheered, despite half of them not even knowing where they were or what day it was. The music began and Roy broke into a surreal robotic dance, spitting the words into the mic like a man having a fit. Max kept nudging me in the back, and some big bald guy with his arms folded on a nearby table said *fucking woeful* loud enough for everyone to hear. His terrified wife, nursing half a coke, sat staring into space. The song came to an end and there was scattered applause, before keyboard porn kicked straight into a lame, elevator music rendition of a Robert Palmer number. *Might as well face it, you're addicted to love...*

'Sounds nothing like the original,' Max grimaced. I giggled inside, but I didn't want to bruise keyboard porn's dream.

We moved on after two pints, and a hen party dressed as pink fairies flooded past, wolf whistling in our direction. One of them smacked me on the arse with her magic wand and they all creased laughing.

The next place was equally as weird, though not quite as lively. A big TV screen had horse racing on, and a pack of desperate middle aged fellas with early 80's moustaches were grunting at the race. They were all shaking rolled up newspapers or betting slips at the screen. The winner came in and they all jeered. One of them said *fucking typical* and swigged his whiskey, followed by a gasp. We ordered two Guinness and propped the far end of the bar.

'Day out boys?' the landlady asked. She seemed very friendly. Must have been seventy.

'Day *and* night,' I laughed.

'Why not, love,' she chuckled, wiping the overspill off our glasses with a sponge.

Max was on a mission. Every time I turned round he'd sank another quarter pint. When I came back from the toilet he had two fluorescent green test tubes in his hand.

'Go easy on them lads,' the landlady smiled, 'the night's young yet, lovies!'

I felt a little spaced when we hit the street. There was a crowd gathering around the entrance to the Tower. I could see a tout offering half price tickets to go up to the top. I looked at Max, who nodded.

'Is there a bar up there, mate?' I asked.

'Is *there*,' he beamed, and I realised he was on another planet. A straggler from a stag party that had wandered off. It was too late anyway. We'd already given him a tenner and had the tickets in our hands. I was quite surprised when the tickets got us through the barrier and into the lift. The rickety click-clack unnerved me as we wobbled up and up, chains clanking, the ground below growing distant through the cracks, and the sound of the wind howling like a banshee.

'I don't like it,' I said, and Max rubbed my head, grinning.

'Awww.'

'Piss off, you patronising fucker!'

At the top it was quite crowded. I had a sudden wave of nausea, and pushed myself flat against the inside wall. Max was hanging over the edge with his phone, taking pictures. The thought of it was giving me hot flushes, and I felt suddenly very vulnerable.

'Go get the drinks in,' Max called. 'I'll be in in a minute.'

I felt safer inside, though the view out to sea turned my stomach. That vast emptiness of the ocean. Staggering really. It felt unnatural being up there, and I couldn't see Ireland after all. The gusts made it ten times worse. The problem with an acrophobic like me is we get the compulsion to jump just to get it all over with. Everything feels bogus up high; as though everything going on around you is a terrible hallucination.

I ordered two bottles of cider, since they had nothing on cask, and Max came in boasting some spectacular pictures of the coast. He had a new iPhone, and I had to agree, the pictures were knockout. He took a selfie of us from above, drinks in hand, then splattered it all over social media.

I didn't mind.

Rumours were rife anyway.

We ended up in a soul bar near the North Pier. There was a mod scooter in the window, and Jackie Wilson was blasting onto the street, which was enough to convince me. Inside the steamy windows a gang of northern soulers, dressed in their soul association polo shirts, were shuffling, slipping and sliding through their slick dance steps, mouthing the words to every song. They had their names on the backs of their t-shirts, which I thought was cool. We were half pissed so it didn't take long to join in. The place was booming, and the music took me to places I loved to go. It was bizarre looking outside and seeing daylight whilst dancing intoxicated, but we grabbed the moment and had a ball.

'Hiya!' I turned to see a striking looking girl with a blonde bob and chessboard dress looking up at me. She was sucking on a straw dipped in a turquoise alcopop.

'Hey.'

'You look like Kevin Costner on *Waterworld*.' We laughed and danced a bit. The girls were a hoot, and I span them round to The Supremes, Dobie Gray, Stevie Wonder, Ray Charles. The girl who tapped me gave me a peck on the cheek then left with her girlfriends, and I turned to see Max on the fruit machine.

'You ok?' I asked. He shrugged.

It felt like we'd been in that bar for days when we stepped out, already drunk, at dusk. We dipped into a cabaret bar for a vodka and soda, but it was pretty quiet and the DJ in drag targeted us.

'The eye candy just walked in!'

He cackled a dirty noise, ramping the volume up on *I'm Gonna Live Forever* by Irena Cara. He brought us a free shot over and asked us what two strapping lads like us were doing in a gay bar. Max let him squeeze his bicep, and he swooned. We never did answer his question.

We left and stopped into a dive takeaway for some greasy chicken wings. The wind coming in off the sea was scattering empty bottles as if they were scampering from something. Abandoned chip wrappers danced wildly in the flurry.

The promenade was alive with neon lights and street vendors and the sweet smell of freshly baked fudge. Max bought a packet of rum and raisin and put a piece in my mouth. Heavenly. A rush of music and bells and sirens all blurred into one mass of noise coming from inside the amusements, and we could hear the rattle of the indoor roller coaster scuttling around the ceiling.

'Why didn't we get fish and chips?' I complained.

'Dunno,' Max said.

We ended up in an 80s themed nightclub, guarded by two massive bouncers in black bomber jackets. One of them was trying to ignore a drunk lad in a Hawaiian shirt screaming in his face. I could see the bouncer's jaw slamming down on chewing gum, inhaling deeply. Rowdy stag parties were out in force, and a day's drinking was descending into a shitshow.

When we got inside, Club Tropicana was thumping from the stack of speakers by the DJ booth, and the place was bouncing to the beat. I was swept onto the dance floor by a plump girl dressed as a nurse, and before I knew it I was in a circle of nurses taking turns gyrating against my crotch. The floor was sticky with spilt ale. Max was dragged into the circle and started thrusting his ass into the girls, who spanked and grappled him, loving it. He was so camp when he danced, especially wasted.

The drinks kept flowing and the tunes had the place whipped into delirium. One rip-roaring classic faded into another, then another. How good were the 80s? As the whole crowd belted out *Somebody To Love* in a variety of faulty, screechy keys, a fit brunette with crimson eyeshadow slapped her lips against mine. Her hand went down the front of my pants and I didn't care. The lights were kaleidoscopic, blinking, strobing. The room looked like it was on the other side of a set of slightly open blinds. Everyone's eyes were closed and in the throes of hedonistic bliss under disco balls, reflecting memories we'd cherish for years. She took me by the hand and led me to the disabled toilet, locked the door, and hitched up her dress.

When I got back to the dance floor Max was deep in animated conversation with a lean guy sporting a tutu. He was ripped, this guy, with magazine cover looks, and they were grinning at one another inanely, white teeth luminous in the haze. Max hadn't noticed I'd even gone. I got two bottles in and took them over, and he took his from me without even looking. I fell back into the crowd, lost in music, dizzied by it all. The girl with the eyeshadow was gone.

After a few more songs Max was gone.

I made my way to the exit and stumbled onto the street where drunken bodies were strewn, and emotional girls in fancy dress and eyeliner running into spider webs were being consoled. I looked around for Max, and called him several times, but it went straight to answer-phone.

This is Max Greaves, I know you're trying to reach me and will get back to you as soon as possible if you leave your name and number.

A very professional, masculine voice.

I took a seat on a bollard across the road, away from the madness, watching the distant Ferris wheel on the South Pier sparkle in the darkness. Some random passed me a cigarette and lit it for me.

'Thanks, man,' I smiled.

The salt air fused with nicotine filled my nostrils and made me feel alive. My eyes were ablaze as though full of dust sized, radiant lights, flashing and fracturing into shifting, swirling colours.

Alive.

That's why we'd come. That's why we were here.

You're a fucking prick, someone shouted, and a sobbing girl rushed past me towards the railings by the sea. A late bus rumbled by.

I hope she doesn't, I thought.

disarray

if every woman in the world
is not enough
to satisfy your
needs

then
you are searching
in all the wrong places
for all
the wrong things

hotels

we will never meet again

you say

so fuck me like you mean it

the phone rings

it's reception

your laundry is ready, sir

staying in the game

take your pills
take your punishment

summon spirits from the floorboards
below

pick the mothballs from
your suitcase it's been
forty years –

lie topless on the beaches of
a thousand magazines

look down from canyons at
shadows
on the walls

flirt with a dozen filthy freedoms
& regurgitate your dreams
into sonnets

ride a wild mustang
down the corridors of
emotion

howl
in discotheques
at
Dawn

think
but only as much as your gut
will let you

stay alive in the shade
(the spotlight
gets way too hot)

open your eyes –

there are human beings
starving naked
sailing across oceans
across borders
across impossible prejudices just
to survive

don't buy into
things you cannot pay for

drop into pirate's cove
because treasure has to belong
to someone

ride through the coal mines
of Appalachia on
the backs of giants
looking for the footprints
of ancestors

visit intergalactic ministries
& show them your true colours

crawl through swamps
with leeches on your skin
fighting for freedoms that are already
          yours   *ours*

listen to Ginsberg

          contemplate jazz

sleep with strangers past their prime

burn your diaries
          deny your age
rock & roll until the grave

drink eldorado rye
               &
shun cheap perfume

embrace the winter afternoon
          like an old lover

take your stardust to far flung places
to the mountains
to the seas
to the jungles & the neon cities

          lie back & wait
for the hand-job of a lifetime from
          angels
          disguised as fools

take your chances
in the alley-ways of festering societies
dictatorships
    political menageries
        constructed realities

bring your stories
home
for a rainy day

listen for heartbeats
as the record turns & turns

watch the finest minds

  dis
    in
  te
    grate

    in the safety of the coffee house

don't be the fool
    that never learns

  at least
pretend

eat with the masters
ride with the hunted
escape from this intoxicating
        hallucinogenic liberty by

running down the dreams
          of children

watch horror movies
until you feel your eyes burn

travel the world as if
                    it was one land

take hollow-brained insomniacs
          by the hand
& lead them
        to a peaceful
                  sleep

be the child on
          the mountainside
when the sun rises
head filled
          with crazy dreams

ignore the sinister phantom knocks
          that midnight brings

          tear
down the beaches of the
greatest wars
          with courage
        lust
          hindsight
                    vision

the masters of such battles
will relive this day
throughout our failed
histories

steer away from the neurotic // psychotic
uptight // short-sighted // pig-headed
yellow-bellied
condescending
egocentric
sociopathic
power-hungry
hypocrites
who wrap their
arms around your
weariness
& fill your head with
promises // assurances
impossibilities // denigrations
mendacities
deceptions // cul-de-sacs
wholly unachievable // unattainable
inaccessible
unreachable falsehoods – delivered
on a plate
made from glittering
white
orthodontic smiles

keep facing forward
keep moving on
don't deny your right

write a book

something to believe in

wake up to the sound
of fingers
massaging your heart
awake

that's how we start our days

when you feel crippled inside
take a moonlight drive

watch the stars
burn cobalt blue

when the skies fall down
in fits of rage
take cover

wait
for the storm
to pass

you'll know when it's armageddon
or maybe you
won't

duck & dive
do your deals
raise hell in a sleepy village

answer
the phone
when destiny calls

take your history
embalm it
          lock it away
only refer to it when the ghosts
          come to retrieve
                    what's rightly theirs

secure a date for
the high school prom before
the silver-spoons of this world
          snap them up

talk a little more

                    think a lot less

walk the cemeteries
      in the rain

avoid decay
          because there's millennia
afforded to us all
to rot & feed the earth

when the liquor in your glass is
          thick // sharp
& cigarette smoke electric blue
                    hold steady

keep your mind alive
don't waste your instincts
on cheap-men's tricks

you can't buy a thrill
or fascination
so don't even try

sit around camp-fires in
the woods
with your fears wide awake

wait for the night-tripper

he's coming for us all

don't linger
at dusk …
… only those without a soul
linger at dusk

listen to bands through walls
strip it all to
skin & bone

never stop looking for friends in
madhouses & parking lots

hide away in pick-up trucks
wait until the lights
are off

carry on until too much
becomes near-enough
enough

cross the great rivers on
platforms of bamboo
head to Memphis with
your country blues
wail
a touch of yabba dabba doo!

breathe the weighty air in hostel dorms
take your sugar
find your groove

cross the badlands solo but
never stop moving
dip a toe or two in hedonistic springs
it'll raise your heartbeat
just a little

keep friday on your mind
hunt sirens in the strobe lights
drink in the narcotic haze
the euphoric saxophone
the one collective beating heart
the music

oh
Lord!
the sweet *glorious music*!

        sanctify
yourself in rivers of belief

feast yourself
on sweet-tooth dreams

        stalk the bars of London town

write to tabloids
        cast your vote

make some extra on the side

never stop

        keep on running

open wide

        the plane is coming

it's all come down to this

let me tell you how
this goes down . . .

i pack my life up
into two cardboard boxes

mail them to England

stick a t-shirt or two
some shorts // three pairs of boxers
three pairs of socks
some flip-flops
one thin jacket
a notebook &
a baseball cap into
a rucksack

i withdraw the little cash
i have
carve a hole into a
hardback book &
stuff it inside

leave my apartment
for the last time

leave the shithole as it stands
// it's no longer
my problem

i take a taxi to the airport
check in
walk through security

never
look
back

that's when you become
nothing to me
but
somebody
that
i used to know

understanding

you took me
          by the throat

too devastated
to scream

then
i knew what love was

park-life

the park was empty but for one woman in high visibility
attire & her dog – a husky with rousing azure eyes,
prowling in the snowy leaves // the muscles in its
shoulders tightened then relaxed, its breath forming
clouds around its overlong nose // she smiled as she
passed, stealing a glimpse at my journal full of doodles,
my fingerless gloves massaging a fountain pen – a gift
                                        from a former love

it was only when she was out of sight that i started to
write; her face difficult to recall

it was nearly dusk when i stood up, a poem or two
lighter // another night of mythic stars closing in like
some grave
          awakening

Father & son

the time comes

when one man & a boy

          become

two men

the flu

you bring the blankets down, turn up the central heating

you're not dying
you laugh, all stars & landscapes & dimples
& butterfly lashes

if i was, at least i'm here with you

you disappear into the kitchen, return with honey &
lemon – your Grandmother's recipe for ailing souls

i watch your hips glide across the lino like a hand-carved
ship from ancient times

now lie back & rest
you say
tomorrow means nothing 'til it's here

roulette

i wonder
if i'll get to see
          80 winters?

70 just doesn't seem enough

any less than 60 a travesty

          i consider this
on mornings when the world
watches breakfast
                    television

trickles
of milk
from bowls of cornflakes
escaping
          the sides
of numb lips
all over
town

i guess it doesn't matter

& it's the high school prom
muddling through steps neither
        of us knew

fumbling breathless kisses

                where do i put my hands?

then dark & dingy backstreets on
        the edge of town

it doesn't even look like a bar from
            the outside
                & we're just so young

down stale stairs
a vibrant collectors den
exchanging glances
        gripping one another with
            fleshy handcuffs

the lights go down
                like years

wraith

my soul shakes
when your memory rattles the keys

humanity

the day i returned
from
North Korea
i cried & cried

i hadn't cried for years
&
i didn't know
if i was crying
for them
or
if i was crying
for me

or
for the boy
on the Pyongyang subway
who stopped
to smile

three degrees of nostalgia

i captured your face
          once

an instinctive click as
          you studied the planets

it's the only thing
i have left

searching

sometimes
i feel like i’m dying
to find
someone
    to live for

tea & biscuits after sex

hearts like drums
damp
muscles limp
& scattered sheets

you reach for the cigs
naked   lean
shards of streetlamp piercing
                your chest
talk about work

            breathless
i turn away & think of home
hear the click
            then steam
listen for the clink & stir
the slop of tea bag in sink
shadows cascading from
            walls

        it's hot
you say
     rousing me

sitting up is such graft

your pubic hair
            so sculptured

TV pumping out true crime
          at low volume

pass the biscuits
i smile
& just like old times
          you do what i ask
                    of you
          with nothing
but tenderness
            & calm

vinyl redux

rid of me
you suffer
the rise & fall
// just replicas

brown dirt trout mask
beefheart apocalypse
she implied
suffering the bends

you're nut gone
in the bush of ghosts
i explain
scaring the hoes

the unknown pleasures
of jagged
l
i
t
t
l
e
pills

bummed
we seek miseducation
  & arcade fire

Dr. Sardonicus
watches
  spiritualized

the indestructible beat
  the *indestructible beat*
the indestructible *beat*
upon dancing feet
as tear-stained pear-drop minds
  return to mono

  damaged
the bright lights tonight
  feel sinister
the weight of these wings
  black
melodrama & the pretty hate machine
  rumbling over off-kilter rhythmic thump
  & Clint Eastwood vibes

the dictionary of souls
the genius behind the madness
  blackouts in Satchidananda
parklife & crooked rain

how will the wolf *survive*?

clandestine
i can hear the heart like
a machine

odelay *odelay*
goats head chief

this is the colour of jazz to come
when things fall apart &
wild honey artefacts
rage in national galleries
for the weak

the bells *the bells*
tubular
fireside love songs
with blues overtones
rapture of sorts
before
surf bubblegum &
the raincoats laughing

when we all fall asleep
where the fuck do we
go?

head littered nightmares
whispery trap-pop
manic blank spaces re-lived
80s heroes through the kaleidoscope
gospel chops &
          village greens in rainbows

Mingus moving pictures
just fevers to tell
the queen of carrot flowers &
                    her hot buttered soul

expensive thrills
          amongst the infamous
the brutal appeal of reading when it's too late
hotline bling
muscular cars & shadows
guitar raunch & the lick of promise
the warped funk of thunder
          & lightning
shifting beds half (in)sane
          splutter like ancient prayers

time in a bottle
motherships & barricades
visionary science-fiction uncut-punk
                              a glide in your stride

extraterrestrial dips in the hip
bending heads & chocolate milky ways
never too much fascination &
                    post-disco romance extravaganzas
two nations under a groove
loose-booty rhythms
hi-fidelity big star city radio
lear jets & fast cash &
                         sweetly eccentric sonic youth
quirks & hallmarks technologically fraught
frazzled freakouts hidden within
                           visions of the world
corners of round rings where
                    reminders are carried

rain dogs // digested shit
the tragic kingdom of the streets
a clove & a hoof
Faustian pacts
signature grungy minimalism
groovy swamp voodoo & the doctor
chemical inspiration in vicious heavy marmalade
                    imaginations of the sun

        the love of my life
strangers   oceans apart
hippie-leaning metal-spawn
occasional germ-free adolescents

his teeth & worn day-glo rags twitching under
          saxophone blasts & chanting

word-of-mouth cults
streams of empty thoughts
earth & sky meeting inside an open hand
class-clown freshmen
          & brain-damaged rhymes
abstract-leaning ultrasuede
                    editions of you & inflatable lovers

openhearted intimacy & lust
kicking out the jams
love // sex // nostalgia
dream highways & liquid swords
          cinematic mysticism
copious kung fu-movie bloodbaths &
the ballad of the midnight parade
strange alchemy & stun-gun distressed falsetto
bar scenes that look like crime scenes
alluringly spooky
          dead-end hookups
boardwalk love songs cut short
rump shakers
pop group at war
New York City serenades
sweetening ballads behind walls of sound
          & respect for the clichés

menacing doggystyle flavoured tales
that harrowing dirty fucked-up slaughterhouse national
anthem for the Nineties

pure synthetic lush electronics
country fables & woozy refined debuts
& stark mystic folkways
& synth-soul landmarks
& basement tapes glued
spider-webbed
so-called standards & friendship anthems
sun sessions & sexy voices

nothing like a prayer
art & commerce
swinging London baroque-gallantry
higher flying balanced on waves
beat junkies
groupies // hustlers // parasites
the turntablist underground
rage within modern vampires of the city
experimental sound painters in
deep deep waters

weird post-college years
old-school block-party showmanship
Dylanesque grand statements hushed & muted
cranked up amps in nunneries

no finesse // just power
jittery slinky social capitulation
with blonde mullet

the world's most done-me-wrong song
firelight between stations
piano-pumping // all-killer no-filler
starry-eyed arena anthems
music in one lifelong spat throughout seasons
austerely beautiful death meditations by
crack crews of poker-faced millennials
cultural rage over high-speed rockabilly
doomed decadent 60s-steeped California romance
hilariously nasty big-bangs
dying in high society amidst rave-y
dance beat whimsical fervour

ecstatic eight-minute-long velvet ropes
battered psyches
& overgrown gardens
supple distinctive tones cushioned by weathered
saloon-numb offshore pirate-radio faces
playing bloodied shady wireless jingles
trashy & thrashy self-harm power chords
centuries-old flamenco music freaking out &
burning cold
bullish palma-pop bravado
lovers by the horns

ancient-modern mash-ups &
                    reshaped barren landscapes
hide & seek drum masterpieces
ducking & weaving & sparring & feeling
native ears &
          stories from the sea
sexual obsessions & romantic disappointments
softened around by marimba
stark postmodern blues
          surging exits howling &
                    a seat at the storytelling table

spoken-word southern interludes
soulful lament to family roots
          nihilism & tentative optimism
stoned symphonies &
          wild fireballs of anger
combustible snippets of sparse tunes
lowdown lemonheads
minutemen & chilly bass line stentorian chants
          the rhythm of doom
harrowing warm-jet dreamy free-form
needles in the camel's eye
jagged glammy art rock disco
civil rights anthems
          &
glistening slo-mo-drone pastorales

posthumous hits written in L.A. motels
all-out passion plays
sweat-dripping vulnerable confessions
classic litanies of alcohol choices
absent Fathers with down-to-earth everyman vibes
life in Harlem
drunken Irish wakes
fattened snatched riffs & radios in a hammerlock
genre-defying effervescence
superstar rule breakers
full moon fever with majestic
northern portraits

visceral sledgehammers
crazy horse rampages
impossibly delicate unspooled powderfingers
surreal political spiel &
collapsing sky guitar roars
random retro access memories
before
despair under sparkly melodies
& haunting farewells
& sequined pantsuits
& bewitching frontwomen
on the edge of breakdowns

Donna Summer futuristic // trippy
mushy otherworldly concepts

last-splash cannonballs
summer over the surfy buzz of sex
chapels of pixie love
        jaw-dropping swagger
kinetic wunderkind roof-shattering dixieland
                boogie-woogie

writings on the wall
        & craft juddering club singles
outcast dichotomies
universal verbal chaos
musical inhibition
        disorienting dissonant yet ensnaring
boundless melodious thinkers
odes to suburban romanticism
                indie-rock innocents
the tough sounds of Lou Reed
harmonised electric-12-string treatments
jangled-up Californication

8 billion volts of electricity
                    down every road
ten songs full of drifters
fugitives // rogues
seminal recordings for Capitol
culled archetypal
        statements & strangers
barren tough-guy individualism

Giorgio Moroder
dancing
& the sweet spot where the *toot-toot* meets the
beep-beep
prototypical concept albums
sunset people & this fantasy of mine
snapshots of rich-boy malaise
the sad bell tones of a celesta
biting ironic sides to surprise monsters
oddball island novelties drenched
in bad acid
taboos // par for the course
mad melody & menace
irresistible precision-engineered hulking metaphors

nothing sells like fear itself

tortured tenderness glowing beside
meat puppet eventualities trapped in lead bellies
heroin unplugged
cosmic quarters inside
houses of the holy
topless diaries fused with classical piano
a love of old soul & Tokyo
the template for the majestic sombre 90s
&
swaying nocturnes lovelorn

epic grandeur melancholy substituting for truth
confessional fake plastic trees
societal dysfunction
hickory winds
vacant rural purists
sweetheart of the rodeo flying high & wide
beneath badland universes & staccato
commodifications of
desire from agit-rappers
barking dogmatic grad students
calling for folk revivals

gentility if you please before
17 minutes of amplifiers screaming
regal hype // pain & resolve
pedestrian lines
small-town polemics
& cold-blooded political science
millennial pop falling wildly in love with witty precision
hate-caked noise assaults &
the ever-darkening megalomania of that
once revered asshole
game-changer

sordid maximalism
catacombs of classic 45s
love & hate in a different time
sardonic tales of sleazy grifters & tin-pan-alley showbiz

primal screams in the valley
smiling through grace & mercy
blasphemous everyman aesthetics
agitated heights
your never-written magnum opus
moptops hiding their love away with cryptic blurts
Bo Diddley beats at 6am
lunacy & alienation
nine-part suites // poignant acid casualties
off-kilter hip-hop bounce
power // corruption // lies
gloriously danceable spunky beats &
right hand drive on pages that could
define you

backward-ball-cap alt-rock kids lost
avant-garde slits in a nutshell
joyously anarchic catchphrases tossed in a blender
mighty blues-mama voices &
pearls on summer lawns
a blaze of freewheeling bloodlines in supper-club swank
wearing rags but keeping your pride
strumming acoustic guitars for spare change
on the streets
wearing coats of many colours
gruelling portrayals of domestic violence behind walls
radical hopes of the anthemic flames &
the raw truths of confronted listeners

tender triumphs
aerodynamic groove machines
footloose masters of war
platinum pipers at the gates of dusk
rubber-punk energy & radioactive matching
jumpsuits & devolution
jaunty confection
        & jilted tantrums
intense affection
thickening skies & perky desolation
looking for a path to greatness
all across the alien nation
across deep houses overflowing
with contentment
along simple entreaties
bartered with
fists-of-fury

the boomin' system in his ride
round-the-way girls cold chillin' over Bob Marley
wholly transporting back to the
gorgeously floating magic-hour
synthetic sham
that is Heaven
or Las Vegas

emotional purge & resurrection drenched in
autotune

unbearable winters & 50 words for snow
whimsy-loving zombies
          purveying noir-guitar maelstrom
creeping slow ambiance
the weight of bass & the mood
        trip-hop cedar trees
                    & bruised knuckles
the Harlem Square Club blown to pieces of a man
perspectives of greatness
croons & strokes
copping a gangsta stance in
                    taut hard-hitting glorious origins
classic interborough beef fests
the Germans & the machines
gussied-up red-headed strangers
          telling riveting & heartfelt tales of murder
                                        & infidelity

French perfected house music as pop
80s guitar cheese &
                    vocoder euphoria
mantras at a dystopian corporate retreat
winky moments in tomorrowland
bare bone blockbusters
maximum heaviness as cinematic melodrama
funky timbale work &
          droning marijuana coming of age
               defected laureate satisfied with silence

flying clusters // loping instrumental gait
          defrilled classic rock

Coltrane - a sheen that made pretty much everything else

overly polished tipsy two-in-the-morning midcareer
                                        reinventions
hazy playgrounds & hair metal
an overturned flowerpot of dead daisies
          confrontationally pessimistic // outraged
merging dancehall & torch ballads
crack addiction // just a dense sample-delic flow
keys to the highway &
              electric brotherly love

falsetto scream igniting unfettered possibilities
critical & commercial gold
          skidding into dissonance
Nashville exiles
          ruffling feathers infectious
the evisceration of Paul McCartney // self-consciously
                                   luminescent // pointedly
                                           embraceable

post-motherhood electronica
radical sympathetic muscle politics
howling one-guitar
          armies making a furor

bombtrack funky fusillades in
roil arena mosh pits
rock & roll powerhouses
vocal-choir gallops & hyperactive ghostfaces
spieling breathtaking drug-rap narratives
sixteen shots in a fish tank
mob movies // pastoral in their intimate flow
hollow slug-eyebrowed cockiness
fame-hating working-class anthems
insolent snarls from the cheap seats
low-fi whispers & sepia-toned librettos
rose parades where
smiles are made
where skull meets spade
where debts are paid
drenched in stony
cherryade

morosely pretty drunken lullabies
down-home stoner country layabouts
writing ultimate outlaw credo
tons of tunes in the can
thrilling eccentrics with single-minded intensity
sandpaper edged cabaret
hot knife fever in the tower of song
dusky commanding band leaders going
through the motions

dramatic set pieces & lilac wine
croaky syrup-addled multiple-personality menagerie
kicking cocaine in Berlin
        it's just sound & vision

NO MUSIC ON A DEAD PLANET

please read the above one more time ↑
& again for good measure ↗

deft expansions of sampling palettes
psychiatric wards & unadorned supernatural devotion
    fame-sucks brags & gripes
intimate bedroom folk & mailed tapes to
        record labels disinterested
neo-classical strings like broken stained glass // boldness
        & abrasion
historic lo-fi synergy
        & bittersweet pangs
walking home in the rain
thrift-store image eyeball-to-eyeball
epochal feminist statements for worldly adults
tears on the dancefloor
desperation & passion & frustration
    body talk
blowing kisses to your muses
space ships in the backyard
cameos & effigies

unapologetic smart-aleck rhymes
three jerks making a masterpiece obscure hilarious
trade-off flows // jerks no more
juvenile delinquent spellbindingly precocious
crossover divas
repression & spiritual release
reporters on the hill
slash & thunder blown wide open
hellbent drumming igniting drama
smashed out of our brains with mythic ambition

gaslighting impossibly explosive
force of nature avenging-angel ferocity
broken world diamond star halos
&
Tolkienesque hippie music
equating cars with sex
stomping on the studio floor
boisterous energy streamlined & free of juvenilia
urban riots in the human heart

kooky garish mainstreet fashion bleeding into
saucy masturbation call-to-arms
blatantly feminist new-wave
brains
visionary fusion of warm & chill amidst
double-murder fantasies

the village is alive with wonder
the village is alive with neo-soul
the village is alive with brown sugar
the village is alive with gentle melodies
the village is alive with private hell
the village is alive with spare melodicism
the village is alive with …   … folk-pop healing
the village is alive with cryptic summers
the village is alive with caustic flagrant homesick
balladry
the village is alive with mariachi-brass drama
the village is alive with my last words
the village is alive with bi-racial cult bands
the village is alive with pathos
the village is alive with raw pleading
the village is alive with Stax

& then
preconceived ideas of mandolin winds
pyrophoric lyrical tirades
autobiographical tales of young studs
sleepwalking through september devastation
terrordome widescreen visions
pimps & butterflies
shanty towns needing subtitles
pressure drop across the tiny universe
Babylon to the new beat
aching death to plankton frat boys & homophobes

vetoed Bach chorales
wry & wounded daydream nations
international clamour over nerves turning toast
        into an array of gnarled hooks
                channelling into scuzzy urban haze
doomy riddles & antennae censorship
otherworldly signals
                trippy jangle

Native American tribal beats &
                sharp eyes for local colour
down & out little Italy hustlers
wedding-band standards
bottle of red // bottle of white
greasy couples half-alive
cuddle bugs reelin' in the years
elusive odes crooning implacably about betrayal
        immorality & sexual domination
a panoply of high-gloss hooks & arresting
                artificial sounds
straight country music
trademark vocal hiccups on springy disco jives
technically limited murmurs
        unspooled secret languages
subliminal approximating hooks or bandages
                        gen x
struggling comebacks before 2,000 inmates
silvery-helium creamy syncopation

sly sense razzmatazz
shabby glamour & post-clubbing hangovers
the most romantic adventures in the world
hippie-angelic blend
murder // execution // incest
synchronicity
distilling complex psychological premonitions
proggy musicianship richly direct &
          dense composition palatable to the mall-rat
                    masses

meditative hard-won truths
androgynous unsanitary dentists
pack in quips & lousy dinners
a phalanx of piqued swagger
true dynasty
melodramatic self-mythologising &
                                        proclamations of sexual
                                                  compulsion

viscera marked by flames
sticky ecstasy
songs of ambition & seduction
spooky acoustic demos &
          black bedtime stories in pulp-noir novels
hard-luck tales of underdogs
enduring gems & moving accounts
a plateful of *Led Zeppelin III*

avant-soul territory raving 'til dawn full
of rootless trailer-trash
an opulent sense of tragedy surrounding Tamplais high
the beauty & the bloodshed
the mistaken reflections laughing
the extended slow-burn
heading north

the unpredictable currents down parallel lines
the perfect synthesis of
raw lives entangled

the priceless demimonde style in
the mainstream

the ethereal strokes of cedarwood

the Crosby in the recipe

the traction in the rain

thoughts of getting out

so strange

turtle doves & ladies
olive branches free & green

the world so crazy

offensive ideas // more denunciations

humour to the voice of a generation

extreme fandom in our era

physical graffiti like a bloated ghost

Arabic & Indian sonorities

invented excess across continents

wailing feedback describing loss

spiritual thirst // revelatory

mere flag-waving mistaken as immortal force
when handcuffed to the bumper
when detached from humanity

college-radio versions of monkeys gone to heaven
bedrock reggae power & ghetto rage
bummed-out kids higher than the seven great peaks
agonised bray in stooge purgatory
war pigs as public enemies
spiritual quests & mythology

slaying everyone with a feather
highbrow-for-lowbrows
the arms race redefining possibilities
settling for mere happiness
long-gone-daddy romps for a life of sin
something as vague as ambiance
ultimate self-pity operas
& Brechtian drama
& suicidal languor
& rock star hubris

far-ranging rococo
the doomy portent of a flood
audacious boundary smashers cross-pollinating
faith & colour

Ray Charles' gospel grit
down & out crying every day
hopefulness hard-hard-won
grinning up our sleeves
more human than ever
learning to feel moving tides
recording on the fly while
the best samples ever put on wax
melt all over white-blues sorcery

caught in a trap of
a million electrical disturbances

industrial corrosiveness
i-hate-the-cops sensibility
righteous indignation of the bourgeois psycho-circus
vanilla-pop broadcasting
two horns & a rhythm section
riding the bonfire momentum
monuments to rock-aristocrat decadence
triumphal autobiography &
soundscapes inspired by David Bowie's
Blackstar

that shake like milk
pondering addictions in swimming pools
ragamuffins jumping from avenue to cemetery
acidic dispatches ringed with distortion
lights that never go out in darkened underpasses flashing
whilst singing from a pay phone

unconventional tunings
being cruelly shunned by the world
electric boots & mohair suits
landmarks of breezy sophistication
glam flash queens & hustlers
rooftops re-imagined
cribbing the lines verbatim
making resentment seem almost fun
MTV-generation gatekeepers
noirish howl of marquee moons

strangled existentialism of double-helix guitar sculptures
friction & brainy art
pure riot-grrrrrrrrrrrrrrrrrrrrl motherhood
Fillmore East cult stories regaled
every single vibration coming from the stage
marching centuries
& telepathy
cut short

sticky fingers on moonlight miles
three feet high & rising
machine-gun blast of unemployment ditties
leftist politics & laughter as currency
record-company shenanigans
heavy rave-ups & paint-peeling love-hound yowls
the template for everything

Parcels in Berlin

communication breakdown when the levee breaks
that pink house in Woodstock
riding shirttails towards motorcycle accidents
family & obligations

dubstep swirl of banjos & talk-box elation
dying wheels on a gravel road by
broken down shacks & engine parts &
busted-down doors & borrowed cash

hard liquor
dignity & a feeling of release
drugs controlling you // dominating the airwaves
argument for sweetness in an increasingly hard world
strings in the face of everything
going down musically with the angels
champagne papis & showstopper spotlights
hard times adjusting to fame
garage-savvy troglodyte grooves
red snapper wannadies by the trail of the deceased
Iggy growls & the band shudders
(there's no question // you wouldn't want any
of whatever he was on)

cheeseburgers in paradise
RIPs too soon
old-school Ann Peebles soul oldies
dragonfly heavy metal
the dead-man with the flaming guitar making it
sing // talk // shriek // flutter // fly
hard-won adult realism
youthful dreams fallen apart & Lennon-style fury
head wrap as trademark
blend of gay camp aliens on Earth
sailor men spangled &
saloon-piano balladry
on-the-spot improvisations brewing futurism

crystal ships & pop-art lighting
self-revelatory vacation on mondays
skirting blasphemy purely nude
unkindest cuts from acerbic
karaoke-tinted fame
drinking sprees & changes in latitude
the relentless logic of the sledgehammer bathed
in plasticine
shaking me all night long looking backwards
racking up Motown
race & geography
darkly self-referential smiles by the American flag
jailors on
d
o
w
n
w
a
r
d

spiral

fiercely compelling highwaymen
with fingers on the trigger &
hatred on bodies

anarchy in the UK
        echoing everywhere
daring aesthetic stunts & pet sounds
                        in the spirit of Beyoncé
sun sessions
        & mystery trains
theatrical lifehouse decimated
epic majesty spiked with synthesisers &
        slinky rascals on high mountain passes
collars popped in strip clubs
                professing insecurities
loveless bloody valentines serenaded by ghosts
                discarding seeds on Kingston doorsteps
        police-siren street beats

show-business veterans
        calm // philosophical // vulnerable
hounds of love exerting ecstatic operatic chirp
        dark rustic revelry
dreaming sheep & waking witches
do-or-die hustles
comic insouciance in underground clubs
the living dead & humble offerings
s   p   a   c   e
saxophone fetish with hearts & tongues
prayerful reflection with explosive catharsis
        the trauma of teen pregnancy

audiophile with an appetite for destruction &
declamatory flow
cooler than a polar bear's toenails
world of the hood // days of poverty
poetic-scat weeks
astral wandering melodies on cypress avenue
blatant let's-do-it-in-the-bath-type things
dance-around-the-maypole pre-battles of evermore &
memories of the night
they drove old dixie down

deep belief
the caffeinated drive of painterly sonic impressionism
fuck & run exiles
inner-space explorations of the madness of everyday life
sleepy-eyed alarm in 7/4 time
fever dreams of underwater electric soul cut
in round-the-clock sessions
under glowing afro bound for demise
excursions to the Delta blues
crosstown traffic & a final burst of spectral fury
the android factory full // sold out
spokesmanship for star time
subtropical // mobb deep
making the club get crunk
clipping off compound rhymes with grace
the holy promise of redemption songs

apartheid inside graceland
under the cherry moon
acrobatic second verses
low-end theory
& people of that nature
getting dope on the double bass
pulling at sound like taffy
violins making frightening white-noise stuff
& that utopian spirit of the 1960s

murderous blues
glittery messianic alter egos &
a whole new school of pretensions
the world moving on a woman's hips
Jimmy Buffet sailing off
ancient-to-the-future rhythm hypnosis
avatars of the punk avant-garde &
polyrhythmic magicians
thin wild-mercury sounds coming loose
contradictory magnificence
the sidelong beauty of the sad eyed lady of the lowlands
funkenstein approved
off-the-wall one-man disco inferno
rock's first sitar solo
resplendently damaged 21st-century torch singers
rising up like a fever
knocking the world sideways // dust to dust
side chicks in the thick of hard bop

dreams about walking under the sea
white albums & voodoo
a hectic panoply of voices on
                    a pleasant valley sunday

Victorian jollity & idle boasts
blackened-riff howls of new wave &
          the heated ennui in the songs of our nation
Warhol-designed infidelity
the love crowd
fledgling Brooklyn rappers awaiting bullets
                    with 360-degree visions of mean streets
rags-to-riches in jungleland
Phil Spector's Wagnerian grandeur
brotherly reliance & alt-rock breakthroughs
abstract electronics
labours & glories from
               the middle passage to
                    the hood
groove paranoia of idioteque national anthem
vomitific literary ambition &
                    shattered limitations of every kind
a Hieronymus Bosch-like
          season in hell
wisdom that has proven fleeting
          like getting a massive eraser out
                    & starting again

the dawn of an uncertain
          decade
free-form radio broadcasts from
                              the end of the world
shattered wind-speed machinations
rampaging ska
heavily in debt & openly at war with
          a lack of dough
racing against the wind // throwing chairs
                         around the room
controversy & the aching sound of triumph bringing
                                   more noise
a piercing sample of James Brown's *The Grunt*

media screed & rhythm engines pumping
          whiskey-soaked churches
                        & corrosive abandon
unconditional survival
Muscle Shoals & expeditions to space
incomparable crossover instincts feeding
          locomotive cadence
LSD at Abbey Road
trippy tape-loop swirls // botulism
          deaf-aid ache
throwing genius titles at Sisters & Brothers unwarranted
swinging sermons
          & heartbreak monuments
the hair on the back of their necks standing straight up

spit on the tracks // blood balance of
contradicting impulses
montage sequence of all people
ballads in Seger mode
territorial pissings // lithium
// conceptual force
deliciously bitter takedown of wealthy complacency
all-encompassing innervisions (again)
wholly unguarded octave-leaping voices
cellophane wrapper secrets
harpsichord
horns
sleigh bells
strings

waiting for the day to close your eyes
aghast at the violence

stumbling around for ideas
scatting & improvising
always smiling on cue (for you)
what's happening Brother?
so mercy me

hardly a dishonest note

i just know this much
is true

sociopath

the air solid
faces just road maps to dead-ends
cold breath &
          flickering lights on empty
               late-night trains

we lie
amongst debris

                    empty
like a shipwreck

looking for my next regret

pretty colours in your hair
everywhere

perfect legs
thighs close
drunk

the strobes light you up

green as the earthchild
orange is burning
indigo cast
yellow lightning
violet arrows all for you

i know we're going home

i don't even have to say what i really mean

i have it
i have it -
that hard loving look

& you come
as i knew you would

there was no other ending

none at all

night theatre

you resonate
where rivers carve narratives

stoic & unyielding
the landscape
            is silent

contours of me
a spectrum unbound
              by convention

        transparent hue

seeing you break
                 away
through halflight

canyons flooded with wind
        hiding secrets

untamed terrain // desolation
mountains
     unrestrained
           & sovereign
   unbound by
        human confines

just your footprints
where freedom is unspoken law

you speak *i had to…*

the muted luminescence
a silent ballet

this theatre

your sanctuary

my purgatory

our wilderness

Mr Zimmerman

whispers
like wildfire through
crowded lanes

a sea of faces in
the bowels of
a bustling city

i see you
on flooded thoroughfares
nestled amid urban calm
landscape of light
against the backdrop
of dusk

& his name in neon:
for one night only

crowds swell along
the promenade
like soft Mediterranean
waves

laughter & disbelief

he's in the building
someone says
& we shudder

queues form
on sunset &
a busker belts out tunes
under the town hall clock

within the confines
of the ornate
Victorian opera house
the air is charged

lights down
brings rapture

silhouettes on stage
crowd feverish minds
until spotlights
reveal rhytides

it's… *him*

then music fills the space
the soundtrack
to lives & love

lucid as hell
images moving so fast

euphoria & catharsis
so close to the bone

then his gaze met mine

a fleeting connection

something that could never last
a crescendo of sorts
unwavering resolve

a hero is not defined by
grandeur or fame
but by hands that heal
& words that inspire

for the flowers of the city
get deathlike
sometimes

death look

The first time it happened I was six years old.

Aunt Nancy had just rescued a really cute Border Collie from the RSPCA, and Mum, being a dog lover, was so excited to show me the pictures. His name was Bobby, and he'd been handed in because his owner, a Royal Marine, had been posted to Iraq.

'We'll drive over this weekend to meet the little fella,' Dad said, ruffling my hair.

We set off early on that Saturday morning to avoid traffic, and reached Colwyn Bay in less than ninety minutes.

I loved Colwyn Bay.

Every time we went we stopped at a little café on the seafront that smelt like baking and cinnamon and happiness, and I had a strawberry milkshake with waffles. The town always looked fresh, like a film set, and the roads around the coast were spectacular to a boy like me, especially with the window down - the calming breeze off the Irish sea lapping at my cheeks.

Aunt Nancy lived alone in a big house, not far from the promenade. It had a huge driveway coated in pebbles, and a stone fountain in the garden. Uncle Brian had been a rich man, I'd heard my parents say, though he was dead now. I still don't know how.

The ivy had grown a little out of hand around Aunt Nancy's large, heavyweight oak door to what was a very impressive four story Victorian property. As she greeted us, Dad promised her he'd sort it out one of these days.

'Oh, Eddie,' she smiled, head tilted, leaning down to hug me. 'You look so grown up!'

The dog had been locked in the kitchen, and bounded down the hallway to meet us when Aunt Nancy let him out. He kept skidding on the wooden floors, and his tail was swirling in frenzied rings. Dad got hold of him first and steadied him, though Bobby was gasping with excitement and trying to break free.

'Well, well, well!' Dad chuckled. 'What a handsome little guy you are!'

Mum also stepped in to stroke him. That's when I first caught Bobby's eye.

I got this instant feeling of nauseating dread. Bobby galloped over to me, sniffing and licking, but I just couldn't bring myself to touch him. Mum and Dad looked surprised, and Aunt Nancy kept saying how friendly he was. She looked really disappointed by my reaction. Dad told me to stroke him but I couldn't even lift my arm. A strange, oppressive gravity seemed to fill the room, and Mum pulled me close. I felt so bad for the little guy that it almost made me cry. Bobby ran back to Aunt Nancy and wouldn't look at me again.

What they didn't know was that Bobby was going to die.

When the call came several weeks later – Aunt Nancy hysterical, Mum running from room to room with the phone trying to calm her down – I nearly threw up. Bobby had collapsed in the garden, foaming at the mouth. He was dead before he even reached the vets. He was barely eight months old.

I saw it in his eyes that morning in Colwyn Bay, and I saw exactly how he was going to go.

Bobby's eyes were already dead.

I heard Mum and Dad discussing it later that night, after the horrible call with Aunt Nancy. She had friends coming over to console her until Mum and Dad could go up to be with her the next morning, though Dad wasn't impressed with having to drive there and back on a Sunday.

'She needs us,' Mum protested.

'I know, I know,' Dad sighed.

'Do you think Eddie knew?'

'Kids are strange little creatures,' Dad replied. 'They have a sixth sense.'

About two years later I was walking into the schoolyard with my friend Kevin. Kevin was a ginger skateboarding kid, and my best buddy. His trousers always hung off his backside, and he liked to paint his school tie funky colours. He was forever in trouble over that. He lived on the next street to us, and we would meet at 8:30am to walk together.

We always made it into school five minutes before the bell for registration, and this particular day was a beautiful morning in early June. Kids were playing football under an already luke-warm sun, and a group of senior girls were smoking by the bike sheds. As they stubbed their cigarettes into the wall and started heading for their block, I caught the eye of the tallest girl at the front. She was thin and a little gaunt, with dyed blonde hair tied up like a pineapple on her head. She was laughing and throwing her arms around until she saw me. Then she seemed to go tense and rigid. One of her friends saw that I was staring, and started shouting at me across the yard.

'Fuck off, you little dick!'

I felt that horrific obscurity pass over me again, and the tall girl at the front seemed to shrink into her own shoulders. I had to steady myself against the wall, and Kevin grabbed me under the arm. I'd gone pale, feint and spaced-out.

'Hey, man. Are you ok?'

'She's going to die,' I said.

A week later in assembly the head teacher gave an emotional speech about the death of a senior year girl called Laura Hancock, who had been run over in a terrible accident in town one evening after school. A photo of that same tall girl I met eyes with in the schoolyard was sat on the top of the piano, and the girls she had been with that morning held their heads in their hands.

Kevin stopped walking to school with me after that, and I found it hard to make friends for the rest of my school days.

Nothing more happened until I was sixteen.

It was a week before my seventeenth birthday, and I'd started college several months previous. College felt good. A fresh start. I had no trouble making friends, and my parents were really proud that I'd aced my school exams even though the last few years hadn't been easy for me. I'd become a solitary boy, and stayed home at weekends rather than mix with other kids. Dad was particularly stoked that I'd got an A* in English Literature. His head was never out of a book, and he often encouraged me to dip into his library and 'exercise the mind'.

One day I pulled a book off the shelf by a guy called Albert Camus.

'Ah, The Outsider,' Dad said, impressed.

'What's it about?'

'Meditations on life and death, son,' he grinned, and then winked.

Mum decided to take me into town for some new clothes for my birthday. On the way to the high street I insisted that we stop off in the independent book store because it sold second hand records, and I wanted to look through their piles.

I'd got into music since spending a lot of time alone. I really liked Pink Floyd and Black Sabbath. As we walked in I heard someone cough, and a young guy, probably about twenty-five, well dressed in beige chinos and an open neck russet shirt, welcomed us. He had a lanyard round his neck that said: *Nick Malloy / STAFF*. He was handsome, with swept back hair and well groomed stubble. As our eyes met I felt my legs go and stumbled into a cabinet displaying the latest releases. Several books took a tumble, and everything went dark.

'Eddie!' Mum screamed, stunned.

Nick helped pick me up, and I had to sit down on the armchair by the fireplace because my head was throbbing. It felt like someone was crushing my temples. Someone had turned the temperature of my brain up full tilt. Nick got me a glass of water, and as I saw him walking back towards me from the little kitchen area out back, I knew.

'You're going to the hospital,' Mum announced, and I didn't have the energy to argue.

The hospital carried out all sorts of tests on me, but everything came back normal. They asked me if I'd eaten anything that morning, or if I was feeling anxious about anything, or if I'd used any drugs. Mum was aghast when they asked that, and pleaded to me with her eyes.

'Of course not,' I said, and they took my bloods for good measure.

Three days later the bookshop burnt down. Nick, who lived in the flat above, perished in the fire. It was the top story in our town, and his face was on the front cover of the local gazette. It described him as a quiet but kind and thoughtful young man who left an impression on everyone he met.

'My God,' Mum gasped as she unfolded the paper, 'that's the boy that helped you that day, Eddie. Remember?'

I remembered alright.

I didn't know what to do. Three times was more than coincidence, but telling anyone would make me sound insane. I found looking people in the eye really difficult. I retired into Dad's world of books, though Mum became increasingly concerned that I no longer hung around with anyone at college. These were supposed to be my best years. Years of discovery, girls, adventure, life.

'Eddie, is everything ok?'

'Fine, Mum.'

'You really don't seem yourself, lately.'

'I'm all right,' I smiled. 'I just don't want to hang out with kids that do bad things.'

She was satisfied with that. I got a hug and a kiss, and I knew I'd bought myself some time. I didn't know what the future was going to bring though. I couldn't go through my life avoiding people.

And what if…? What if one day I saw that look in…? It didn't bear thinking about it. I couldn't comprehend that.

The year was 2002, and I was twenty years old. I'd got over my fears – university had helped me do that. I was studying Literature in Sheffield, which thrilled my Dad. He was never off the phone discussing my assignments, suggesting extra reading and lending his ideas. It was nice to be honest. Books were our bond, and I was glad that it made him happy. It made me happy too. I loved to read.

Mum missed me more, since I was an only child. She'd always been desperately maternal. At any opportunity she'd be over that Snake Pass to take me out for dinner, or buy me some shopping, or check that I hadn't fallen for an unsuitable girl.

I shared a house with Patrick and Barny.

Patrick was from Kilkenny, drank like a fish, played guitar like Van Halen, and wore a thick sheepskin coat at all times, even indoors. Barny was also a heavy drinker, an obsessive gamer, and a Ramones nut. He wore black nail varnish and a nose piercing, which made my Mum stop and look twice.

Patrick came home one time after uni and said: 'I need twenty quid off you both, pronto.'

Barney looked up from his deep Playstation meditation and scowled.

'What for?' I asked, bemused.

'Because, gentlemen,' he swaggered, 'we are going to a gig!'

That summer we took the train from Sheffield to Manchester for the Move Festival at Lancashire Cricket ground. The tickets Patrick had blagged were half price from a friend of a friend, and we were off to see Paul Weller, the Modfather. I really liked his music, and Patrick was well into The Jam. Barney would go anywhere there might be a full session on the ale involved, and it was very jovial on the train where many concert goers were crammed together with cans of ale and sandwiches and lots of friendly banter.

The act we were really looking forward to was Joe Strummer.

Strummer was third on the card of support acts, and was due on at 4pm. We were drunk by then, and had just had a wonderful time bouncing in the mosh pit to Shed Seven. Rick Witter, the lead singer, even put the microphone to my mouth as he came into the crowd, and the whole of Manchester heard me sing *we're just chasing rainbows...*

We were clamped on the front row when Strummer walked on, and as he hooked his classic black Fender Telecaster over his shoulder I caught his eye. He caught mine, too.

There it was again. That instant out of body experience.

The sound of the crowds chanting evaporated into a strange, vaporous drone, and all the strength within me seemed to splash out onto the floor into the piss and the beer and the grime. When I started to claw my way out of the crowd, bouncing from chest to elbow to face, I heard Patrick's voice.

'Where you fucking going, man? It's just getting going!'

Joe Strummer died of a heart attack later that year at the age of fifty. It had been months and months, so I'd hoped it would never happen, and that I'd finally broken the spell.

Things were never the same with Patrick and Barney after that, and they both moved out of our shared house in time for the third year. I had to rent a room in a converted convent in a rough part of the city, but that was ok. I could be a ghost, and nobody bothered me because they knew I was in my final year and needed to study.

One night I was up writing an essay until 3am – a study on the emasculation of Torvald in Henrik Ibsen's *A Doll's House*. It got to the point where I could barely keep my eyes open, so I went to the bathroom and started to brush my teeth. As I pulled the cabinet door back, I took a good long look at myself in the mirror and that feeling came once again. I held on to the sink and waited for it to pass.

Everything was different after that.

I thought a lot about Mum and Dad.

I decided I'd call Mum in the morning and tell her that I loved her. I thought about Aunt Nancy, Kevin,

Patrick, Barney. About what this life actually meant anyway.

I couldn't sleep, so I threw a hoodie on and took a walk to a nearby park; watched the darkness gradually consumed by particles of light, and the street lamps of the city flicker off from my vantage point above the rooftops.

I should have felt terror, but I didn't.

I felt calm.

Unexplainable calm.

That morning I told my Mum how much I loved her, and she asked me what had happened. Dad got on the phone and asked if I needed money. I told him no. They came over the next day, worried, and we spent a lovely weekend together. They stayed in a hotel near Meadowhall, and we even partied a little on Saturday night in one of my favourite pubs where a band called Grenade played classic rock covers.

When they left I wasn't even emotional. Everything had reached a finality that was out of my hands. Knowing was easier than not knowing.

And yet, here I am, telling you this story all these years later.

manuscript

my words
are
burning
in the bin outside

but that’s alright

i
was burning
when
i
wrote
            them

previously published

sabbath day
reasons for sharing
provincial town taxi rank
rest home
why didn't anybody tell me?
now for forever
morning before the flight home
time
village supermarket in january
were all published in *Marias at Sampaguitas* during a period as a regular contributor

the poet
was previously published in *The Cannon's Mouth: Issue 28*

last tuesday
was previously published in The *Interpreter's House: Issue39*

to follow
was previously published in *Fire (Summer 2008)*

that day on the seafront
was previously published in *Borderlines: Issue 44*

so many questions
was previously published in *Black Bough Poetry: Issue 1*

we are made of
was previously published in *Black Bough Poetry: Issue 2*

i woke up thinking i was Miles Davis
was previously published in *The Cabinet Of Heed: Issue 25*

bandages
consort
(de)generation
were previously published in *AYASKALA*

vacation
in cities
'you' is not reserved for two
the old man
were previously published in *Dodging The Rain*

for the purpose of experiment
was previously published in *Porridge*

secret
late october
craving
were previously published in *The Curly Mind: Issue 8*

why
was previously published in *Elephants Never*

oasis
was previously published in Bending Genres

isn't it time
one night in Phuket
were previously published in *Vamp Cat*

some people have no poetry
was previously published in *The Broken Spine Artist Collective: First Edition*

headlines
was previously published in Issue #2 of *Recenter Press Journal*

the bones of dogs
was previously published in *The Broken Spine Artist Collective: Third Edition*

day 1
day 3
were previously published in *Otherwise Engaged [#5]*

day 6
was previously published in *Marias at Sampaguitas*

day 8
was previously published in *Red Planet Magazine [#7]*

day 11
was previously published in *ang(st) - the feminist body zine*

day 12
was previously published in *The Pangolin Review – Special Covid-19 Issue*

day 13
was previously published in *Pendemic* and *Feral: A Journal of Poetry & Art*

day 16
was previously published in C*ajun Mutt Press*

day 18
was previously published in *Doghouse Press [#2]*

the journey
was previously published in *Poems Of Adventure Anthology*

day 31
was previously published in *Feral [#2]*

day 32
was previously published in *Streetcake [#68]*

day 41
was previously published in *Big City Lit*

day 48
was previously published in *Sin Fronteras / Writers without Borders [#25]*

day 67
was previously published in *The Organic Poet*

day 69
day 70
were previously published in *Sage Cigarettes [#4]*

day 73
was previously published in *Global Poemic*

day 81
day 82
day 83
were previously published in *U-Rights Magazine*

shame
was previously published in *Burning House Press*

somewhere in the countryside
such a pretty picture
were previously published in *Words for the Wild*

dissident
this is what they've done
music used to live here
that thing they can't abide
were previously published in *Cleaning Up Glitter*

put that record on
was previously published in *BOLD*

northern towns in winter
journey to Snowdonia
were previously published in *last exit*

cross country
was previously published in *3 Moon Magazine: Catalyst, Issue 1*

it's only belief
was previously published in *Allegro: Issue 20*

the last night of our lives
was previously published in *anti-heroin chic*

ruminations
was previously published in *Barren Magazine [#9]*

melancholy
was previously published in *Shot Glass Journal [#27]*

things can change
was previously published in *Three Drops From A Cauldron: Issue 27*

at dusk in the city
was previously published in *Constellate Literary Journal*

songwriting
was previously published in *POETRY NI+ Panning For Poems: Issue 10*

reflected in puddles
was previously published in *Dear Reader*

unreachable
was previously published in *Dream Noir*

all i'm thinking about
was previously published in *Elephants Never*

building nests in the country
seasons
were previously published in *Eunoia Review*

college nights & days
was previously published in *Ghost City Press*

Hemingway
it's never too late
were previously published in *Crêpe & Penn: Issue 2*

recovery
was previously published in *Light Through The Mist - A Shorthand Anthology*

music
was previously published in *Blossom In Winter: A Collection of Poetry*

decay
was previously published in *Iceberg Tales*

itinerant
was previously published in *Re-Side: Issue 1 - Anonymity*

market day
was previously published in *Silk + Smoke: Issue 1*

the skylark & the boy
was previously published in *The Fictional Café*

i think i'll call it morning
was previously published in *The Fiction Pool*

supernatural
was previously published in *Foxglove Journal*

so did i
was previously published in *Turnpike Magazine [#5]*

for the purpose of experiment
was previously published in *Porridge*

head in the clouds
was previously published in *Dreamcatcher: Issue 22*

staying in the game
was previously published in *The Whiskey Tree: Untamed Identity (Wave 1)*

tea & biscuits after sex
was previously published in *The Whiskey Tree: Untamed Love (Wave 1)*

night theatre
was previously published in *The Whiskey Tree: Untamed Nature (Wave 1)*

Mr Zimmerman
was previously published in *Stage: Poetry in Response to Live Arts*

Paul Robert Mullen is a poet, writer, musician, radio presenter, podcast host, lecturer and traveller from Southport, near Liverpool, England. He best describes himself as a sociable loner - young at heart and old in mind. He is the co-founder, occasional guest editor and regular contributor to *The Broken Spine Artist Collective*, an internationally acclaimed journal of poetry, photography and art. Paul is also a widely published poet across a vast array of international magazines, journals, e-zines and anthologies, including *The Interpreter's House, Barren, Heron Clan, Dreamcatcher, Borderlines, Ghost City Press, Burning House Press, Wellington Street Review, Allegro* and *Porridge.*

Paul has had four collections of poetry published. Three collections, *curse this blue raincoat* (2017) *testimony* (2018) and *35* (2018) were published by Coyote Creek Press, and *disintegration* (2020) by Animal Heart Press. A conglomerate anthology with fellow Southport poets Alan Parry, Mary Earnshaw and David Walshe - *Belisama* - won the 2020 Dreich Alliance competition and was published in 2021. Paul's first collection, *Issues, Tissues & the Senseless Comic*, was self-published in a very limited run.

A former University and College Lecturer, Paul is an Executive Producer in an education technology production company these days. He enjoys playing in bands all around the Liverpool area, reading, researching Bigfoot conspiracy theories, vinyl records, country pubs, skiing, ghost stories, boxer dogs, roast dinners, coastlines and cricket.

Robert Sheppard has published many books and has appeared in many anthologies of both criticism and poetry. *The Meaning of Form* (2014) is available from Palgrave, his episodic history of linguistically innovative poetry, *When Bad Times Made for Good Poetry* (2011), is out from Shearsman. Earlier essays were published in journals such as *New Statesman*, *Times Literary Supplement,* and *PN Review.* His poetry includes the long poem *Complete Twentieth Century Blues* (Salt 2008) and a selected poems from Shearsman, *History or Sleep* (2015). His recent transpositions of canonical sonnets, the 'English Strain' project, is published as *The English Strain* (Shearsman 2021), *Bad Idea* (Knives Forks and Spoons 2023) and *British Standards* (Shearsman, forthcoming). A kind of autobiography is

Words Out Of Times (Knives Forks and Spoons 2015). A book of essays on his work, *The Robert Sheppard Companion* (Shearsman 2018), outlines these and other activities and publications. He has edited collections by writers as different as Lee Harwood and Mary Robinson. Sheppard lives in Liverpool and is Emeritus Professor at Edge Hill University, where he ran the MA in Creative Writing for far too many years. He enjoys performing his poems and has been known on occasions to sing the blues and play the harmonica.

Website: **www.robertsheppard.blogspot.com**

Alan Parry is a poet, lecturer, and the dynamic Editor-in-Chief of The Broken Spine. He holds a BA in English Literature and Creative Writing from the Open University, and an MA in Popular Culture from Edge Hill University.

Parry began his poetic career with the lauded debut, *Neon Ghosts* (2020), and continued to make waves with the award-winning *Belisama* (2021) and *Echoes* (2022). His latest collection, *Twenty Seven* (2023), both interrogates and celebrates the enduring legacy of Jim Morrison.

In 2023, Alan's spoken word debut, *Noir*, premiered at the Morecambe Fringe Festival, further establishing his status. Under his guidance, The Broken Spine actively nurtures a vibrant literary community with events and online initiatives. His present projects, *The Whiskey Tree*, a series of thematic slimline anthologies, underscores his continued commitment to supporting poets and their shared spaces.

Website: **www.alanparrywriter.co.uk**

Emily June Kelly is a Graphic Design Artist and Illustrator based in Liverpool who works in Education Technology. Graduating in 2020 with a degree in BA Illustration from The University of Central Lancashire, Emily went on to complete a masters in MA Graphic Design & Illustration from Liverpool John Moores University in 2021.

Emily is a specialist in both traditional and digital illustration, and has worked on a vast variety of media based projects, from the stage to literature to charity endeavours and museum curatorship. She enjoys gigs, painting, camping, travelling, reading classics and tequila.

Website: **www.emilyjunekelly.com**

recommended reading

Anthologies

The Broken Spine Artist Collective: First Edition (2020)
The Broken Spine Artist Collective: Second Edition (2020)
The Broken Spine Artist Collective: Third Edition (2021)
The Broken Spine Artist Collective: Fourth Edition (2022)
The Broken Spine Artist Collective: Fifth Edition (2022)
BOLD: An anthology of masculinity themed creative writing (2023)
The Whiskey Tree: Untamed Nature (Wave 1) (2024)
Stage: Poetry in Response to Live Art (2024)
The Whiskey Tree: Untamed Love (Wave 1) (2024)
After House: Beat Culture Made New, (2024)
Fusion: 2024 (2024)
The Whiskey Tree: Untamed Identity (Wave 1) (2024)

Chapbooks

Neon Ghosts (A. Parry, 2020)
The Mask (E. Horan, 2021)
Holy Things (J. Rafferty, 2022)
From This Soil (C. Bailey, 2022)
The Keeper of Aeons (M. M. C. Smith, 2022)
Four Forked Tongues (L. Aur, S. Filer, B. Lewis & E. Kemball, 2023)
Modest Raptures (E. Rees, 2023)
Surviving Death (K. Houbolt, 2023)
Twenty Seven (A. Parry, 2023)
Loggerheads (L Heuschen, 2024)

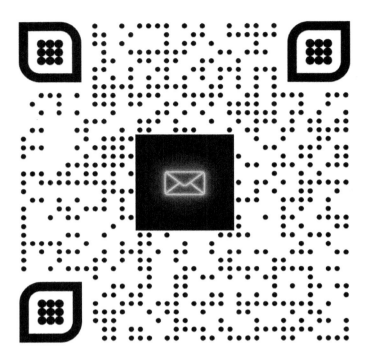

Printed in Great Britain
by Amazon

50633541R00270